Wa
Distance

To Kath, Mark, Phillip,
Helen + James

from

Martyn Wright

MARTYN WRIGHT

ISBN-13: 978-1515297680

V1.1

DEDICATION

To my wife, for encouraging me to do it and remembering who everyone was.

CONTENTS

THE FIRST BIT - NAVARRE AND RIOJA

We left our house on a cold and foggy Tuesday morning in April in the north of England, just after Easter, on foot with boots, backpacks and walking clothes, just as we would be for the next 8 weeks. We'd decided to walk the 4 miles from our house to the station. A friend of ours had said, when we had first told him of our plans to walk the Camino de Santiago, that a pilgrimage should really start from home. He was more 'old hippy' than religious, and was intrigued by our plans. He was saying exactly what I had been thinking. I had even got as far as sketching out a plan in my mind, starting by walking to the cathedral at Chester, following the River Dee to Llangollen, the Offa's Dyke Trail through the Welsh borders, over the Severn Bridge, the coastal path, then Exmoor and Dartmoor, to Plymouth. Then the ferry to Santander in Spain and the Camino del Norte all the way to Santiago.

But then I woke up. We were both impatient to be abroad, hear other languages and be in another world. But flying Ryan Air seemed so wrong. So unreal, so disrespectful to the idea of 'pilgrimage' so unpoetic. Some would say unspiritual, but I hesitate to speak of such things. So we compromised on travelling overland to the start of the walk itself at Saint Jean Pied de Port, at the foot of the Pyrenees.

We followed an old railway line, now a footpath, to the underpass under the main road between our house and the station. I'd been there many times before, but on this day, in the fog and in an excited and suggestible state of mind it seemed for the first time significant, like this underpass was the gateway between the small town where I'd grown up and now returned to, and the outside world, which we were entering. The edge of my comfort zone. The back of the wardrobe to Narnia. Leaving the Shire.

The train flew swiftly down to London, arriving bang on time. I never expected that. I knew there had been rail works on the line over Easter, and expected them to overrun like they had after the New Year. I had allowed hours and hours of extra time to make the international connection, so we had time at Kings Cross to sit and watch the world go by as we waited for our Eurostar to Paris.

The Eurostar arrived on time in the late evening in Paris. I'd never booked tickets on Eurostar before. It was a pleasure to see all the arrangements I'd made falling into place. Much more satisfying than seeing them all go wrong. We walked briskly through the Gare du Nord. You should always look like you know where you're going in a strange city even if you don't, especially in the Gare du Nord at that time of night. I've never actually been successfully robbed. The last time anybody tried was on the Paris metro about 10 years before, on the occasion of my 50th birthday. My assailant was foiled partly by my habit of travelling in trousers with lots of zip pockets, front and back, up and down. By the time he'd worked out where the wallet was my large friend had arrived. Actually he was mostly foiled by his own incompetence. I felt like joking 'have you done this before?' as I grabbed his wrists, but then I thought his mate might be standing behind me.

I sort of knew where we were going because I'd looked it up in Google street view the night before. Not a good idea to be wandering around vaguely at that time of night, wearing backpacks. We soon found our overnight room in the Rue Mauberge. Rachel was very concerned about the possibility of bedbugs on the camino, quite rightly. We were lucky enough never to encounter that problem, but we were always on guard. Funnily enough, of all the places we stayed, including all the albergues, the place where we most saw evidence of a past bedbug infection (by inspecting the mattress) was the hotel in Paris. We didn't want to take a chance right at the start of the trip so we declined to enjoy simply sleeping on the sheets and instead used our sleeping bags and liners on the bed. We had bought these specially for the trip, pre-treated with permethrin to ward off the bed-bugs.

*

In the morning we returned to Gare du Nord, at a

safer hour, and took the metro a surprisingly large distance (about 5 miles) across Paris. The morning commuters looked just like they do on the tube in London. Bored. To us it's a curious phenomenon, but they have to do it every day, twice. We had thought about walking it, we had enough time, but we wanted to make certain of catching the TGV. I had never checked into a French train before, there were a lot of unknowns, so again we decided to leave ourselves masses of time at the Gare Montparnasse. There was no problem, except that there appeared to be two trains to two different places leaving at the same time from the same platform. This seemed to confuse the French passengers as well as us, which was reassuring. It was of course two virtual trains within one physical train, and the train split at some point, which did raise the possibility of being in the wrong part of the train.

We found our seats and the train pulled out. We felt excited to be abroad, hearing another language all around us, everything going according to plan. The guard seemed satisfied with our e-tickets. Soon we were hurtling through the French countryside at 200 km/hour. We passed Poitiers, close to where a friend of our lives, then Angoulême. Everything was going so well...

There was a loud bang and an immediate but steady application of brakes, causing us to slow gradually and grind to a halt. In a tunnel. Rachel hadn't heard the bang, she'd been in the loo at the time, so I thought the 'bang' must have happened close to where we were sitting. Men with torches (flashlights) came along the track, looking underneath the train. After about half an hour we started moving again, but much more slowly. This was worrying, we had to catch a connection from Bayonne to Saint Jean to reach the accommodation we had booked for that night. I had allowed extra time for the connection, not taking the one suggested by the website but booking on the following one, giving us two and a half hours to make it instead of just half an hour. But would that be enough?

We stopped at Bordeaux. A whole gang of workers arrived outside the window where I was sitting, looking intently at the part of the train underneath my seat. Some of them went under the train with wrenches. They came back out with what looked like slightly twisted metal grills, and threw them onto the platform. They didn't put anything back. One of them took photos with a tablet of the underneath of the train where we were sitting. Someone who looked like a boss took out a mobile (cell phone) and talked to someone for about 10 minutes. Then they all stepped back from the train and we started moving again.

I reckoned we were about 2 hours behind schedule at this point, so there was still a good chance we could make the connection if nothing else went wrong. A different kind of countryside flowed past after Bordeaux, more foreign. Instead of cow pasture and arable farming there were extensive pine forests growing out of what looked like sand.

We were indeed 2 hours late at Bayonne, which was fine, we made the connection. This wasn't a train but a bus. There was some serious work being done on the railway up to Saint Jean. It must be a beauty, one of the great railway journeys of the world when it's working. It follows a river up into the mountains. Such lines are prone to serious problems like the river deciding to change course, or the mountains falling down.

The bus visited all the train stations en route to Saint Jean. For the first time we saw other 'pilgrims', *peregrinos*, people from many countries. Our travel plans were working out just fine, others had been delayed by the French air traffic controllers' strike, some arriving from America and having to switch unexpectedly from a connecting flight to the train from Paris, some were a day behind schedule already. As we left Bayonne we saw the Pyrenees for the first time, a barrier of mountains across our path, green in front of us but covered with snow further away to the left, stretching to the east in a straight line, just like they are on a map. I spend a lot of time looking at maps. Sometimes I take a good map with me to bed and just read it.

Saint Jean reminded us of Parthenay, a small heavily medieval town where our friend lives near

Poitiers in France. In fact, it was visiting Parthenay that had put the idea of the camino into my mind. Parthenay was on an old pilgrim route that fed into the Chemin de Paris at Poitiers, only a days walk away (from Parthenay). Our friend had a little house bang on the medieval main street, and it was there I first saw the scallop shell, one of the symbols of the camino, carved into walls or on ancient doors, and a sign outside a church indicating that it was 1489 km to 'Saint Jacques de Compostelle'. The seed was planted in my mind. It wasn't Martin Sheen in the film 'The Way'. I'm not knocking that film, we enjoyed watching it shortly before we set off. But it wasn't what inspired us.

Like Parthenay, the heart of Saint Jean is the medieval main street running from the Porte Saint Jacques to the Porte d'Espagne, down which hundreds of thousands of pilgrims have walked over the last 1000 years. Our lodging for the night was in Gite Ultreia, right on this street. Ultreia was a word we were to see along the way, often the name of a café or albergue. It means 'further', or 'onwards' in medieval Latin. It's what pilgrims used to greet each other with in the old days. Nowadays it's the more laid back *'Buen Camino'.*

We were easing ourselves in gradually to the pilgrim way of life. We shared a room with only 2 other pilgrims, and the beds were regular single beds, not bunks. We were booked in for two nights. We didn't exactly need a rest after the journey, but again I was being prudent in case we were badly delayed. We'd booked the first few nights on the camino, as far as Pamplona, to make the first few days easier. We didn't want to lose these bookings just because we'd got held up somewhere.

Besides, it was right to spend a whole day in Saint Jean, settling in to the camino, exploring this historic small town set amongst high green mountains. We easily managed to fill the day, walking the town walls, looking at everything. The official start of our camino was the 'Pilgrim Office'. Here we got our *credencials*, the cards you need to have to be admitted to the albergues. These are stamped each day when you arrive, and possibly additionally in churches and cafés along the way, and provide proof when you eventually reach Santiago that you have indeed walked all the way. This proof is shown in the Pilgrim Office in Santiago where you receive your *compostela,* your certificate. For me, the *credencial* is the important thing, covered with interesting stamps from all the places you've stayed, reminding you of all the places you've been.

It was early in the year, and it had been a cold late winter in northern Spain. I was concerned about the snow on the pass. I really wanted to take the high route, the Route Napoleon. This was the historic route, and I like snow, up to a point. The alternative was a long slog by a road up a deep valley where the sun never shines, to Valcarlos. Besides, we had a booking at Orisson, which is on the Route Napoleon. I'd been checking the weather reports every day leading up to us setting off, temperatures were just about above freezing on the pass and it seemed it should be feasible, but you never know, the accumulated snows of winter might be too much. Also, I feared the authorities would err on the side of caution and issue a blanket ban on anyone walking that route in case some inexperienced walker, as many pilgrims are, lost their way in the snow. No is always the easiest thing to say.

I was impressed by the man in the Pilgrim Office. He was very specific about where the snow was, how deep, and the condition of it. He spoke to us in English. He had been there only a few days before and was obviously an experienced mountaineer. I felt he had sized us up, noting we were wearing sturdy boots with ankle support but walked comfortably in them, and that we had a compass. He told us the pass was open, but had only been open for a few days. There was snow, not too much if you're wearing good boots. The only thing was, we should not take the sharp descent straight on down after the Col de Lepoeder but should instead take the road to the right, down through Ibaneta. I fully intended to heed his advice. He gave us our *credencials* and wished us a hearty *Buen Camino*, the first of our journey.

What really took some getting used to was managing our stuff. We had hiked and backpacked before, but we seemed to be out of practice. The art of managing in a small corner of a shared room, with all your belongings in the rucksack. At first whatever I wanted to do - washing socks or having a shower - seemed to involve getting everything out to get something at the bottom of the pack and then putting everything back, then realising there was something else I needed, and where was it anyway? It's so much easier in a private room when you can just empty out all your stuff and spread it around, but that wasn't going to be our style on this trip, at least not most of the time.

We got better. You need the same things every time you arrive at an albergue - things for washing yourself and clothes, clean clothes for when you come out of the shower, bedding of course - sleeping bag and liner. It's quite simple really. The main thing is to have as little as possible, both to keep down the weight on your back and to feel organised. Even so, our packs weighed about 10kg each. Some say that's too much, but we were already being minimalist. It wasn't summer - we needed a sleeping bag and some warm clothing, decent waterproofs and pack to hold everything, plus a pack liner because for some reason no rucksack is ever waterproof.

We were easing ourselves in gradually to the walking as well. The very first booking I had made was the albergue at Orisson, only 8 km from Saint Jean. Only when this was confirmed did I make the other arrangements - the cheap advance train tickets, the hotel in Paris, the nights in Saint Jean and also Zubiri and Pamplona. Orisson is the only place to stay between Saint Jean and Roncevalles, on the other side of the Pyrenees. If you don't stop there, then your first day will be the longest and hardest of the whole camino. A massive 1400m of ascent (and descent) on a day when you're not seasoned to carrying a pack, or wearing boots, or walking up or down hills. It could break you before you've got going. People have died on the first day, typically men of about my age.

*

We started early next morning. We didn't have far to go, but we wanted to get into the habit. The street was quiet outside Ultreia. A statue of Saint Jacques as a pilgrim, with a staff and a gourd, looked down on us as we passed under the ancient Porte d'Espagne, an arch imbued with far more history and beauty than the one we had passed under to leave our home town two days before. It had looked down on many millions of pilgrims over the last thousand years. On the other side as we left the old town and looked back was a statue of the Virgin Mary looking protectively over departing pilgrims.

We climbed up through green countryside, forest and sheep pasture, with lambs in the fields at this time of year. It looked like Wales. Although 8km isn't far, we had to climb 800m vertically, and we weren't used to the packs. We had prepared by going to the gym in the months before setting off, which was good, and of course our new boots were broken in, but we weren't used to the packs pressing down on the shoulders. Still, we had plenty of time to take breaks with our packs off and reach Orisson about midday.

We were greeted by a small, dark, very lively young woman. She was simultaneously checking in several groups of people, explaining things (shower tokens, laundry, meals etc) in at least three different languages, none of them her own (she was Basque) while continuing to serve passing hikers with coffee, sandwiches and beer. I couldn't possibly have done the job she did, she had so much energy for people. We ordered our evening meals, one of them vegetarian, and our packed lunches for the following day. There was absolutely nowhere else between here and Roncesvalles.

The dorm was tricky. This was the only place to stay and they had understandably squeezed in as many bunk beds as possible, so there was very little room to unpack even a few things. It became second nature later in the trip but at this stage it took some thinking about. I said to Rachel 'It's like the first day of being in the army'. I don't know why I said that, I've never been anywhere near an army. An American voice boomed from across the dorm 'That was a long time ago'. It was Mike, a retired colonel from the US army, 70 years old, tall and fit with short cropped hair.

Rachel realised she'd left a lightweight thermal blanket behind in Saint Jean. We were still getting used to moving on every day. This was the one and only time in the whole trip either of us left anything behind. Luckily, the very capable hostess was able to sort it out. Viviane from Brazil, one of the two other people we shared a room with in Saint Jean was also staying in our dorm here, and she was having her bag transported. There was still time to phone the *auberge* in Saint Jean, who had discovered it by now, and the company that was to transport Viviane's bag to Orisson and have them pick up the blanket at the same time. Sorted.

We passed the afternoon in a very leisurely fashion, having pegged our washing to the line behind the *auberge*, underwear flying in the wind beneath the Basque flag, sitting drinking hot coffee on the terrace built to take advantage of the spectacular view of the Pyrenees, and getting to know fellow pilgrims. There was Mary-Ellen. I noticed her because she was an American drinking tea, and we were Brits drinking coffee. Actually we'd already met her on the way up. She was only 5 years older than us, but had had a heart operation, and so paid to have her luggage transported each day. You can do that and so only carry a light daypack, but that does exclude you from some of the albergues, the ones run by the local authorities (*municipales*) or churches (*parroqias*). These are the cheapest places to stay, often run by volunteers. They like to feel they cater for real 'pilgrims', and do not wish to be taken advantage of by 'tourists' looking for a cheap holiday. Orisson, like most of the albergues where we stayed, was a 'private' albergue. Actually we were still in France so it was an *auberge*.

By now there were mountains all around us. The Pyrenees no longer lined up in a neat straight row. Only the higher mountains far to the east seemed to be covered in snow. We couldn't see much snow nearby, or in the direction we were heading. This turned out to be deceiving - there was plenty of snow ahead of us but it was hidden from us by the shape of the hill, as is often the case in mountains. We were right to spend a lot of time there looking at the view. The next day would be foggy, and we would be happy just to find the path.

It is clear to me now that the evening meal at Orisson was the most memorable of the whole trip. The were about 50 of us, seated on benches at two long tables. The dark girl ran round serving food and red wine and keeping everybody happy. Reversing the stereotype, the man, Jean-Jacques the proprietor, was in the kitchen single-handedly producing a three-course meal for 50 people, and catering for vegetarians and other special requirements. There were many other places where we all sat down together for a communal meal, and they were all good for getting to know people. What made this special was that we each had to stand up, say who we were, where we were from and something about ourselves, perhaps why we were doing the camino. This was very effective at breaking the ice, not that there was any. There was plenty of wine to assist in this. Everyone had to eat here, there was absolutely nowhere else to go, and it was right at the start of the camino. We kept contact with people from this meal, off and on, at least as far as Pamplona, generally most of the trip, and in some cases all the way to Santiago.

The guests here were mostly our age, despite the fact there were all ages on the camino, presumably because younger people were more likely to go from Saint Jean to Roncesvalles in one day. They were mostly English speaking, I don't know why. In fact, about half were American. We were sat opposite Mike and his wife Mary. She was about 20 years younger than he was, and both looked young for their age. Mike was not the sort of person I would normally sit down to dinner with, or even meet socially - a retired colonel with a seven-car garage and a gun collection back in Colorado. He'd been through Vietnam as a young man. Both were devout Catholics, undertaking a genuine pilgrimage. Not at all the conservative stereotype, he was at age 70 on foot in strange land, vulnerable and surrounded by people from other cultures and backgrounds. I admired him.

We met Peter and Harry, two brothers from Holland. They were easy to spot on the trail later, both tall, walking side by side and even dressed the same - they'd bought their gear for the trip together. They struck me as both being strong but peaceful, spiritual men. They walked at the same pace as us, and did the same stages as we did. I knew they could have walked faster or further but chose not to.

One was a prison guard, the other worked in a DIY shop.

There were Dave and Sue from Australia. Dave introduced himself by saying he was there to be a sherpa for his wife, which was true, he carried almost all her stuff in his pack. Dave and Sue were to be there at our last camino meal in Santiago six weeks later.

There was Viviane from Brazil whom we'd already met in Saint Jean. She teamed up with Reyne from California. Rachel was pleased to meet Reyne, a fellow vegetarian. Viviane was a devout catholic, Reyne perhaps had more of a hippy spirituality, but they seemed to get on well. There was Guido, the outgoing young Italian, and Dieter and Gudrun from Germany. And many others.

There was another woman from Brazil, not far from us on the long table. I had noticed her on the climb up, and been concerned about her. She was clutching a plastic bag with her lunch in it, her pack was small but with lots of things hanging from it and she was wearing trainers. She seemed inexperienced, and stopped a lot, unsurprisingly on the steep slope. How wrong I was. I heard her telling someone it was her fifth camino. That made her the most experienced pilgrim of us all. I asked her what changes she had seen since her first camino 20 years before. She said there were so many more people than ever before.

The growth of the camino in modern times is a phenomenon. The heyday of medieval pilgrimage was the 12th and 13th centuries. The Black Death dealt it a serious blow in the 14th. I can see the towns along the way would have become uneasy about receiving streams of unwashed, diseased pilgrims when plagues were sweeping across the world. By the 1980s, only a few hundred pilgrims a year arrived in Santiago. The revival has come about without any conscious effort by the Catholic church or the Spanish tourism authorities. In fact, it seems to have come as a surprise to both. The camino was declared a world heritage site by UNESCO in 1993, and the tourist authorities in Galicia promoted it at that time, but otherwise the camino has built up its own momentum. Pilgrim numbers are now back up to medieval levels, about a quarter of a million people a year and rising.

*

The next morning we got ready, slightly more efficiently than we had the day before, had breakfast in the *auberge* and started slowly up the single track road. It was cold and foggy, but we soon warmed up walking steadily uphill. It felt like the adventure was really beginning. We all walked at our own paces. In the fog it often felt like we were alone on the hill. I was concerned to spot the turning off onto the dirt-track that leads to the col. This was the place in the movie The Way where the son loses his way (in the fog) and perishes. It would have been easy enough to find, even if Dieter hadn't been there waiting for Gudrun. We passed a trio of 70 year old Americans, Nancy, Bentner and Jim. We'd met them the night before, and would see them again on and off for the rest of the camino.

There was a cross at the turning point, a memorial to someone who had indeed perished there, no doubt the inspiration for the story of the movie. Every day we would see one or more of these crosses. Not that that's any cause for alarm, millions have walked this route over the centuries. Some of them would have died even if they had stayed at home. I'm not at all morbid, but it does make you wonder, for each of them, what was the story. What happened to them, did they die here or was this just an apt place to put the memorial? The memorial typically just gives the name and the age of the pilgrim. Worryingly, it was slightly more likely to be less than my age rather than more. I researched this on the internet when I got back. Some were heart attacks (mostly men of my age or older) or road accidents (mostly cyclists). The story that sticks in my mind is that of an unnamed Italian pilgrim diagnosed with terminal cancer, who died on September 21st 2004, at the cathedral in Santiago, after completing his pilgrimage.

We were walking with John Brierley's excellent guide book to the camino subtitled 'A Practical and Mystical Guide for the Modern Day Pilgrim'. That may sound pretentious, but I quite like his style. His maps aren't maps like I am used to, the very detailed Ordnance Survey maps we have in the UK.

Not maps you could measure distances or take compass bearings from. That wouldn't be appropriate on the camino, and may not even exist in Spain. It's the best marked trail in the world. Just look for the yellow painted arrows everywhere. His maps are crowded with information about albergues, cafés, hotels, churches, *fuentes* (drinking water fountains) and all the things pilgrims care about. They give the distances between villages, roads, forks in the paths numerically in kilometres. The text alone would not be sufficient to find the way. It doesn't need to be, the way is so well-marked, but the text is helpful, particularly where the route-finding is a bit tricky.

The camino is the subject of the oldest tourist guide-book in the world, the *Codex Calixtinus.* It was written in Latin in the twelfth century. The first four books are on religion, culture and history, but the fifth and final book is simply a practical guide to walking the very same route. You could try following it today, if you could read Latin. Some of the *albergues* or *hospitales* mentioned in the book are now a pile of stones in the middle of a field. Some might be under a car park in a city. Some have evolved into modern *albergues.* Certainly most of the churches and cathedrals are still there, enlarged over the centuries. I only found out since we came back, while checking facts for this book, that the author of the *Codex Calixtinus*, Aymeric Picaud, came from Parthenay, the town in France where I first had the idea to walk the camino. Spooky.

Book four, part history and part legend, tells the story of Charlemagne's battles against the Moors. It's a long story, but Charlemagne founded a strong Frankish kingdom in a time long before England or any other west European nation even existed. From this power base he was able to turn the tide of the advance of Islam and the Moors in Spain. However, he failed to win the hearts and minds of the Basques on the way, probably because of what would now be called collateral damage inflicted on their capital city, Pamplona. As his army was returning over the Pyrenees to what is now France, by what is now the Valcarlos route, the Basques attacked his rear-guard, destroying it in the narrow mountain pass, and killing his right-hand man and great Frankish hero, Roland. All this happened only a short distance from where we were walking. If our route had been closed we would have had to walk on the Valcarlos route ourselves. These days we would have been in more danger from Spanish truck drivers than seriously disgruntled Basque warriors.

The fourth book also describes a legend of how Saint James then appeared in a dream to the Emperor Charlemagne, calling him to liberate his tomb in Santiago from the Moors. According to the legend, Saint James showed Charlemagne which way to go by showing him the Milky Way. Most of us in the modern world never see the Milky Way, simply because of light pollution in the night skies of our towns and cities. Everybody would have known where it was in those days. It arcs across the night sky from east to west, the direction of Santiago from Saint Jean. In French the camino is sometimes called the *voie lactée,* the Milky Way. In Spanish, the Milky Way is called the *Camino de Santiago.* Even 'Compostela' means 'field of stars'.

The *Codex Calixtinus* not only documented history, it shaped it by exhorting millions to go on pilgrimage to Santiago, and also by exhorting knights to go there to clear the way, by force if necessary.

We ascended into the fog, clutching our modern guide-book, faithfully following Brierley, higher and higher, encountering more and more snow. A stone plaque announced it was only 765 km to Saint Jacques de Compostelle (cover photo). At some point we crossed the border into Spain. We walked in snow for about 2 km, about 10-20 cm deep, OK in our boots, sometimes in forests of bare trees, sometimes crossing sloping ground. The snow was soft, the temperature was above freezing. Snow doesn't panic me. Ice does.

I made a mistake. No excuse really, I should have estimated the time I should have arrived at the road at the Col de Lepoeder from the distances and elevations in the guide-book, although it's hard to say exactly how much the snow is going to slow you down. Years before I had worked for a couple of years as a walking leader. But I got casual, it was so easy just to follow the well-trodden path through the snow. I had promised the man in the Pilgrim

Office I would not take the steep route down from the Col de Lepoeder, the camino itself, and that I would instead turn right and take the road down into Roncesvalles. We'd been going downhill for a minute or so, chatting to each other, when it dawned on me. We're going downhill, we must have passed the Col. We'd come down fairly steeply through somewhat deeper, soft snow. Nothing dangerous, it was a steady gradient, we could see the trodden route in front. I had thought it would be obvious when we came to the Col. I remember the spot now. The tiny 'road' had completely disappeared under deep snow. The camino signs of course pointed straight on. Everybody in front of me followed these signs, and each other. There had been foot-tracks in other directions, and one of them must have been made by people taking the road route to Valcarlos.

I had followed people in front of me. They were moving downhill faster than us, and were now out of sight. No-one had followed me. The train of people behind me must have switched to the other track, down the obliterated road. We were alone. We seemed to have already come down the snowiest and steepest part of the allegedly dangerous route. If that was all there was to worry about we could just carry on down. I didn't fancy going back up. That would cost a lot of time and effort. But one possibility bothered me - that we were not coming down the official camino route but another GR (*grande randonée*) or forest track down the wrong side of the mountain. That could cost seriously more time and effort, especially without a good map. For the one and only time on the camino, I used my compass for real. The track was descending in roughly the right direction. We decided to press on down.

If we were on track, we were following a route down which more history has flowed than any other I can think of. We had plenty of time to think about others who had descended this very track through this ancient forest. Napoleon rode this way into Spain on his white horse, Marengo, with the *Grande Armée* of 100,000 men in 1808. It couldn't be too bad, they must have manhandled cannons and ammunition wagons down the steep bits. The medieval pilgrims came this way in droves. They wouldn't have seen the beech forest as a beautiful natural place to be, as we do. They would have seen it as dangerous, the forest concealing bandits and wolves. The Romans put a lot of effort into improving the road here. Their road was later used by armies of Vandals and Visigoths, and later a Muslim army on its way to destruction by the army of Charles Martel at Poitiers. What a different world it would be if that battle had gone the other way. The route is almost certainly prehistoric, although there are no written records from before the Romans.

Three young Koreans appeared above, descending our way, and quickly caught up with us. I don't think they had any idea at all where they were, much of a map or any compass, but it was nice not to be alone. The track continued to descend, well out of the snow and most importantly, in about the right direction. For mile after mile through the forest there were no camino signs, hopefully only because there were no turnings off, and there were no long views to give us a fix, although the fog had lifted now. I kept a wary eye on the compass. The young Koreans just crashed on ahead through the forest. The direction of the track swung more definitely to where I thought Roncesvalles was. It was several miles before we came out of the forest to a track and saw, oh joy, a camino sign. In a few hundred metres we were in Roncesvalles.

We paused for a beer in the sunshine at the Posada hotel. This was my first attempt at speaking Spanish in Spain, a chance to see how well I had learned from Duolingo on my computer at home. I was immediately corrected by the barman. He probably does this ten times a day. No-one asks for a *cerveza* in Spain, at least not on the camino. They ask for a *caña*, a glass of beer.

The old Augustinian monastery has received pilgrims since at least the 12th century including, according to a 13th century poem describing it in Latin 'Catholics, Jews, pagans, heretics and vagabonds, the good and the wicked'. I guess we were somewhere in that list. The place was as vibrant as it would have been in medieval times. Perhaps 200 people were being checked in by a throng of volunteers. It seemed like I could hear every European language, and many from Asia too. It may have looked old on the outside, but it had recently been refurbished and was almost futuristic on the inside. The huge dorms were divided by partitions into little cubicles, each of four bunks. The showers and toilets were all at one end of the dorm. The dorm was mixed, but with separate showers and toilets for men and women, as was to be usually the case on the camino. The bunks, the lighting and the facilities reminded me of a modern North Sea ferry. It was the only albergue that did not provide blankets and there were two-metre snow drifts in the courtyard outside, but that was OK, it was heated enough, though you did need a lightweight sleeping bag.

We ended up sharing one of these cubicles with Dieter and Gudrun, our German friends from Orisson. There was quite a queue for the men's showers at that peak time. I was standing in the queue wearing only my lightweight trousers, clutching my travel towel, flannel, and little bar of soap. The shower room was badly steamed up. A tall Norwegian man had the bright idea of opening all the windows to let the air through. Good for dealing with the damp, but there was snow outside, and the mountain wind played on my nearly naked body for about 10 minutes until I got to the front of the queue. Luckily the shower was hot enough to cure my nascent hypothermia.

The *hospitaleros* working there were from Holland. They directed us to where we could wash our clothes and get our evening meal. Pilgrims were still streaming in off the mountain. One of the last was Mary-Ellen. We were glad to know she had made it. It was the first mountain she had climbed since her heart operation.

We went to the church of Santa Maria, stepping forward with the other *peregrinos*, even though we are not Catholics or even very religious, to receive a special blessing for our journey to Santiago. Immediately afterwards was dinner back at the Posada, a 'pilgrim meal' at a big round table. The two Dutch brothers, Peter and Harry, were sitting on one side, a Korean family on the other. The food was a pleasure for us in Spain (although it can be a bit tricky for vegetarians) but it must have been a bit alien to the Koreans. They didn't seem to eat the *postres*, the sweets/deserts, saying they were too sweet for them. The puddings are the best part of any meal as far as I'm concerned.

*

Lights-out in the big dorm was enforced automatically by computer at 10pm. You can't argue with them. We were awoken gently in the morning by the sound of Gregorian chanting, at about 6am. These are the hours of a pilgrim - you need to be up early and on the road around sunrise to get to where you're going before it gets too hot. The difference in temperature between morning and afternoon is phenomenal, far more than at home. It was still early in the year, but we were soon to encounter hot afternoons. These hours put you at odds with the rest of Spain. Spain seems to get going late in the morning, the shops don't seem to open before 10 am. They take a long and late lunch, siesta and dine late. Pilgrims have their communal meals around 7 pm. The Spanish, unless they too are *peregrinos,* don't eat until about 10 pm. In Madrid whole families go out to eat about midnight.

Unusually, there was no breakfast in the albergue. We extracted some coffee from a machine and set off in the early morning twilight, pausing for a photo in front of the road sign announcing it was 790 km to Santiago. That's funny, it was only 765 km yesterday. The cafés in the first village we came to, Burguete, took the early morning flood of half-awake pilgrims in their stride. We had our first breakfast in Spain, the first of many early morning *cafés grandes con leche* with *zumo de naranja* and a kind of croissant. These *zumos* were orange juices freshly squeezed by a remarkable machine. The barman just fed big juicy Spanish oranges in at the top and the machine peeled them, squeezed out the juice and kindly filled our glasses. And these were no ordinary oranges, throughout Spain they were the best oranges I've ever tasted anywhere, except possibly Morocco.

The weather was perfect, cool, mostly sunny and the clear air allowed us to see now along the Spanish side of the Pyrenees, the higher peaks far away to the east covered in snow and shining in the early morning sun. We were walking through high wooded hills, and we could feel ourselves pulling away from the Pyrenees as the day wore on. The guide-book warned us of the steep descent into Zubiri, our resting place for the next night. By now we were beginning to get the measure of the guide-book. To us it wasn't steep, just a regular, admittedly rough track down from a mountain. Nevertheless, I heard a shout behind me and turned to see it was Mike. He had turned his ankle on a rock in the path and cried out in pain. This was a tough guy, not one to make a fuss if he could help it. I went back to see how he was. He seemed OK, and his wife Mary had arrived by now to dispense tender loving care, so I carried on. I only ever saw Mike and Mary once again, on the streets of Pamplona, but I know through the magic of Facebook that they did make it all the way to Santiago. In fact they made it a few days faster than we did.

As we entered Zubiri on the bridge over the Rio Arga, Guido the Italian was waving to us from the balcony of the pension he had already checked into. We found our albergue, *El Palo de Avellano* - The Hazel Stick, that we had booked before leaving England, checked in, made our beds, showered and did our washing. The bunks were further apart than they had been the previous two nights, making it easier to manage. It was important to get the washing on the line by 4pm for it to be completely dry before sunset. It's even more important to remember you have washing on the line and retrieve it sometime, otherwise you'll run out of clothes long before Santiago.

Chores done, we went for an afternoon cup of tea in the sunshine at the excellent Café del Camino. We sat at a table with Patty from the USA, whom we knew from Orisson, and two people we hadn't met before - a Swiss lady and Didier from France. Didier spoke only French and after two days of relative solitude was desperate to talk French with someone, even an Englishman. My French is limited, school French supplemented by visits to France, Linguaphone when young and more recently Duolingo, and also a French conversation club we belong to, where we are pretty much the bottom of the class. Nevertheless, Didier and I managed to have a conversation.

Didier had been to Liverpool, to watch his team Paris St Germain play Liverpool FC at Anfield. Whenever we travel abroad I always tell people we're from Liverpool. I don't really know Liverpool well or go there often, but it's only about 10 miles from where I grew up and where I now live, and everyone, at least of our generation, has heard of Liverpool, thanks to the Beatles, and the football club. The city has declined in the last 50 years, but people still remember its days of glory.

He had walked the Chemin du Puy, all the way from Le Puy in France to Saint Jean the previous year, about the same distance as from Saint Jean to Santiago. This is one of the four main pilgrimage routes across France that connect with the Camino Frances, as our route from Saint Jacques is called in Spain. He had chosen that route despite living in

Orléans, which lies on the Chemin de Paris, another one of the four historic routes, because of the *beau paysage* (beautiful countryside) on the Chemin du Puy.

The tables were turned at the evening meal where everyone at the table apart from us and one young man were French. Didier could talk to his heart's content, it was our turn to struggle. The one young man was Arun, a PE teacher from London. I told him I had completely got over my childhood prejudice against PE teachers. Indeed, he was nothing like any PE teacher I had endured at school. He was sensitive and intelligent, as well as fit and strong. Naturally, we never saw him again as our pace was no match for his.

*

We were getting used to the routine. I'm not normally a morning person, far from it, but on the camino I was happy to get up soon after 6am and looking forward eagerly to getting my boots on and setting off for another day's adventures. Perhaps it was the early morning Spanish coffee.

Tous les matins nous prenons le chemin
Tous les matins nous allons plus loin
Jour après jour la route nous appelle
C'est la voix de Compostelle
(words from the song 'Ultreia' by J. Claude Bénazet)

Starting that early in April the trees and bushes were still as bare as in winter, though the sun was strong and the days were well long enough. Walking the camino as slowly as we did we saw the day by day changes in nature as first one kind of tree, then another came into leaf. Wayside wildflowers were as pretty as a painting, far better than my cultivated garden. Cowslips and primulas here in the early days, and swathes of red poppies all the way across Spain. The same flowers as at home, but many more of them, presumably because of the less intensive agriculture. They stood out against a background of fifty shades of green, with big splashes of yellow from the fields of rape. The colours seemed brighter here, either because of the effect of a mass of colour or because of the brighter sun.

Everyday on the camino, all the way from Saint Jean to Santiago, we heard the sound of cuckoos. Again, this is a sound that was once common at home but is now unusual. Mary-Ellen remarked they sounded exactly like a cuckoo-clock. She reckoned they didn't have them in the States, or at least the part of California where she lived. I'm not sure this is correct, but anyway she had never heard them for real before. I'm not sure when I last heard a cuckoo-clock. It must have been in a Disney cartoon.

That day, as we approached Pamplona, we experienced heat we wouldn't feel again for another four weeks, despite the advancing season. We took the new alternative route into the city, alongside the river, through a park. It was hot in the middle of the day, but not as hot as the city streets. Crossing the Puente de Magdalena over the Rio Arga we viewed our first Spanish old city, the spires of the cathedral shooting up above the solid city walls. We entered through the massive gates of the Portal de Francia and made our way, following the brass scallop shells set into the pavement, to the Calle Mayor. We caught sight of Mike and Mary in the crowd, for the last time as it turned out, but Rachel was dying for a wee and keen to find the hotel we had booked, which was on the far side of the old city.

We had planned a rest day in Pamplona. It seems to me a lot people don't plan rest days at all, unless they're sick or injured. The albergues take a similar attitude, only allowing you to stay one night, unless you have an excuse. But there are famous cities along the way, well worth looking round properly, while you're there. Besides, it's a long time to go without ever standing still for a day, getting a grip on where you are, and breaking a rhythm that could become too automatic.

On our rest days (there weren't that many) we would stay in a double room of some kind in a basic hotel or pension, glad of the bathroom, space to unpack and leave our stuff while we looked round the city, and privacy, which is in short supply on the camino. Maybe it's more important for couples to have days like that. I was fairly sure we would get as far as Pamplona, maybe with twinges and the odd blister, even though I was not so certain we would succeed in doing the whole thing. Actually we had nothing wrong, so far so good. One down side of rest days is that you can lose touch with people who don't stop. But then again, you meet others.

*

We had an early breakfast, to keep in the same rhythm, and went out to explore the old city. We discovered that the rest of Spain, including the cities, is on a very different timetable from pilgrims. The city was quiet, very quiet. No shops were open until 9 or 10 am, and there was no traffic in the old city. We walked round the walls, something we always like to do in old cities, if they still have walls. At about 10 o'clock there was a flood of white vans in the narrow old streets, carrying essentials like fresh bread, and plumbing. I had to jump into a doorway out of their way a few times, caught out by the change. This was Pamplona. Later that day I wrote on Facebook I had been 'running with the white vans'. Pamplona is of course famous for the 'running with the bulls' in July, something to be avoided if you're a pilgrim as the accommodation is booked up. We walked around the outside of the *Plaza de Torros*, where someone had posted their contribution to the debate about bullfighting '*Ni arte ni cultura*' - 'neither art nor culture*'.

We entered our first cathedral on the camino, collecting an extra stamp in our *credencial* and seeing the first of a number of massive gilded altarpieces. We went in search of a vegetarian restaurant that Rachel had found out about before leaving home. It was hard to find. Brierley's guidebook only shows a fraction of the streets that actually exist, necessarily given the size of the book, and there was no sign of the restaurant at street level. It was upstairs through a door that was locked most of the day, with no indication of when it would be open, and looked like it just led to private apartments. I got the feeling that buying vegetarian food in Spain was a bit like doing a drug deal. Nothing was advertised, you just had to know numbers to ring.

We did solve the puzzle eventually, and the food we had for lunch, at Sarasate, was excellent, even for a non-vegetarian like me. It was difficult to find any food at about 7pm when we wanted to eat later. The Spanish may sit around drinking something and watching the world go by at that time but they don't try to eat a proper meal until about 10pm, too late for us *peregrinos*. Luckily we teamed up with Martin and Mercedes, a Spanish speaking couple from London, in Pamplona on a city break. He was English and she was originally from Mexico City. They were able to find out what food was available when, and what was suitable for Rachel, far more easily than I could.

*

As we left Pamplona the next morning, passing the university, we walked for a while with Abi, an

Iranian-American, and his American wife. He was one of only two Muslims we met doing the camino. He described himself as 'born a Muslim'. He was interested in history and old world culture, which is probably the reason for his walking the camino. It didn't seem appropriate at first meeting to enquire further about being a Muslim on the camino, and we didn't see them again after we lost contact later in the morning.

We climbed up across open countryside towards Alto de Perdon. The ridge was crowned with wind turbines, and we could feel the wind rising as we approached the summit. Some people object to wind farms but I don't see what the problem is, a bit of a whooshing sound that's all. To my senses, roads and heavy traffic are far more of an offence. The very summit was left free to give pride of place to the famous statues, steel silhouettes depicting a line of medieval pilgrims struggling into the wind, pennants fluttering above them, with the inscription '*Donde se cruza el camino de viento con el de las estrellas*' - 'where the way of the wind crosses the way of the stars'. The 'way of the stars' was our way, the way indicated on a dark night by the Milky Way.

From the summit I looked at our way ahead across relatively flat land to the south-west. I could spot the next three villages mentioned on Brierley's map but that night's resting place, Puente la Reina, was just out of sight in the haze, and possibly in a dip in the land by the distant Rio Arga. The descent was marked with an exclamation mark in the guide-book, the second one since the Route Napoleon. It didn't seem steep to us, just rough.

Puente la Reina seemed quiet in the afternoon. We found an albergue, luckily getting an 8-bed dorm just to ourselves. This was in early April, this sort of thing happened much less often later in the trip. The *hospitalera* spoke good English, and she told us of a café down the road which had a veggie pilgrim menu, and this turned out to be true, much to Rachel's delight. Spain, at least on the camino, was not turning out to be so hard for vegetarians as everyone said. The small town consisted mainly of two parallel streets, a wide modern one with albergues, cafés, shops and all things modern and a medieval *calle mayor* leading to the very old (Romanesque) bridge that gave the town its name. The bridge seems so huge and strong it's hard to believe it's over 800 years old.

*

The next morning we set off in light drizzle down the *calle mayor* and across the old bridge over the Rio Arga. We stopped in a café in the first village we came to, watching the news and weather on the ubiquitous big TV. The weather report spoke of '*temperaturas de verano*' - summer temperatures. Not what we wanted to hear, but these were in south and centre of the country, not where we were. The presenter was very agitated about *tormentas* where we were, thunderstorms along the border between the hot and cold air-masses. Lots of flashing zig-zags over where we were walking.

The land wasn't as flat as it had seemed from the Alto de Perdon and the villages seemed to be on the tops of the few hills that rose above the plain. We walked on and off with a man I dubbed the 'whimsical Spaniard'. He would get bored with the main track and wander off through an orchard, rejoining the way later. His wife was around somewhere, plodding on some distance behind him. He picked a bough of blossom from a fruit tree, which he said was for his wife, but broke off the tip and presented it to Rachel.

We crossed the Rio Salado, whose poisonous waters are warned against in the Codex Calixtinus. It's still true 800 years later. As we sat on the bridge and rested our feet, the whimsical Spaniard crossed by walking on the parapet on the edge of the bridge, flirting with the dangerous drop into the river. Our destination that day was the Casa Magica at Villatuerta. This was the last of the bookings we had made from the UK, and the first of the vegetarian albergues. It had a relaxing hippy ambience, with incense and things from India. The young woman at reception spoke only Spanish, really forcing me to use the limited Spanish I had learned, which was good. The food did not disappoint - vegetarian paella.

After finishing our chores (the routine sock-washing) we went to the common room. An

American doctor offered to share his bottle of red wine with us. A woman came into the albergue with about a dozen children, aged from about seven to ten. Rather a lot of children for one woman, I thought. She came over and asked us if we would mind joining them and speaking English with the children. Why not, I thought, we have nothing urgent to do. She was originally from that village but had spent a lot of years in Australia and spoke English fluently with an Australian accent. She had returned to her village and worked as a primary school teacher. She offered us drinks if we would join her, not that she needed to, it would have been mean to refuse such a point of contact with the local culture.

Rachel and I each sat at a table with about half a dozen children. The teacher sat at my table and filled our glasses with wine. I felt slightly embarrassed to be drinking wine in front of such young children. Neither they nor their teacher, who kept my glass topped up, batted an eyelid. The boys asked me simple questions - what is my name, where do I live. The girls were more reticent, I asked much the same questions of them. Can you imagine that happening in the UK? A primary school teacher going into a pub, persuading a strange man she has never met before to interact with the children in her care and plying him with drink? No, I don't think she was being irresponsible, I think we're just paranoid.

*

The next day we were venturing into the unknown, beyond what we had researched from the comfort of our own home. We skirted the town of Estella, which is no doubt very interesting but it was early and the centre was off our route, but we did pass the Bodegas Irache. As we left Estella a man asked us in Spanish where this was, and I was just about able to direct him. Like many other places on the camino, there is a *fuente* there, in this case a tap, offering drinking water to passing pilgrims. More unusually, in fact uniquely, here there is a second tap, dispensing red wine. Free. As much as you want. Well, not quite, there are notices about not abusing this generosity and a CCTV camera to embarrass any such abusers. The Bodega limits the wine to 100 litres every day. When it runs out, it runs out. Still very generous. When you think about it, if you get there early in the day, you've got a lot of walking still ahead of you, possibly under a hot sun, so take it easy. If you get there later, it has probably run out. We had some, Rachel more than me, as usual. The man who had asked us directions arrived. It turned out he could speak perfect English, and was from the University of Barcelona. After the drink, we walked on together. I learned a lot about the history of Spain from him.

We were aiming for the albergue Hogar at Villamayor de Monjardìn. The distinctive hill of Monjardìn with the castle on top reared up from the plain in front of us, a clear beacon. Today was a very short day, only about 13km, but the alternative would have been to press on to Los Arcos and then face a long day to Logroño. Hogar is run by Christian *hospitaleros* mostly from Holland, although the young woman who checked us in, Sarah, was from the States. She had been there quite a few years, and spoke Spanish fluently. We were checked in outside on the terrace. We got to the front of the queue and sat down. Sarah asked us if we wanted a private room or to go into the dormitory? I was going to say dormitory, but it had been quite a few nights in dorms. As we sat down Rachel and I both caught sight of and recognised Australian John heading straight towards our albergue. We looked at each other. We didn't need to say anything. 'Private room', I said. Australian John's reputation preceded him. I must say he was a nice bloke, but people were talking about him up and down the trail. There's snoring in every dorm, but there's snoring, and then there's snoring. Australian John's snoring would wake the dead.

The private double room, with shared bathroom, was only a few euros more. It would have been worth it just for the privacy, and well worth it for a night's sleep. I wouldn't know what to say to Australian John - it's not his fault. He didn't even know he snored before he came on this trip. He soon found out. Every night people would wake him up to tell him so. I suppose he should take single rooms, but that would cost him a lot more than he had expected to spend per day. He never shared the pilgrim meals, either because he was afraid of interacting with people he might later fall out with or, more likely, simply couldn't afford them, and ate food he had bought from a shop instead.

There was half an hour's meditation (optional), with some Christian prayers, before the communal meal. Rachel was very happy with her veggie option. Naturally, the important thing is to ask about veggie alternatives when you check in, not wait until the dinner has already been cooked.

Our American friend Mary-Ellen was disturbed that night by Australian John, even though she was in the next room to him. Nevertheless she remained kind and tolerant towards him. That may have been the problem. Mary-Ellen liked us, and often headed to the places we were staying. She told Australian John where she was going. Australian John liked Mary-Ellen (who wouldn't like her) because she was the only person who was kind to him, so he aimed for the places where she was going.

*

We planned to walk to Sansol, another hilltop village half-way to Logroño. We got there early under a threatening sky, and had a beer in the bar, deciding whether to stay there or press on only another mile down across the river and up the hill on the other side to Torres del Rio, where there was a choice of three albergues. Clearly a storm was building, but slowly and so we decided to press on. We made it across the river and checked into one the albergues. The bunks were very close together. We didn't worry about that, we'd been spoilt by a run of half-empty dorms. The thunderstorm broke with lightening and heavy rain and naturally everybody piled into the nearest albergue, which was soon ours, as the one at Sansol only had 20 beds. The room was packed with dripping pilgrims and wet packs. The albergue was really a dorm attached to the village bar, except it wasn't actually attached. Well, the showers and toilets were attached to the dorm, but to get anywhere else like the bar or any common area away from the crowded dorm you had to step out into the pouring rain, raising the question of whether or not to change out of wet walking clothes into the dry and only other set of clothes, and whether to put your boots, waterproof coat and trousers back on every time you went to the bar.

The *hospitalero*, actually the barman, spoke only Spanish. As soon as we'd checked in I heard an impasse behind me between him and a group of four French people about my age who could speak only French. For the first and only time in my life I found myself attempting to interpret back and forth between Spanish and French. An interesting exercise, I'd never tried that one before. I hope I didn't leave too much confusion in my wake.

*

After a surprisingly good night's sleep we were packing to set off, almost the last as usual, when I heard someone banging on the door of the toilet block, from the inside. It was a young man I had seen before in the dorm. He sounded a bit distressed. I tried the door from outside, but couldn't get the latch to open. I told him to hang on, I was going to fetch the *hospitalero.* There was a crowd of people around the reception desk. This was urgent, I had to speak to him quickly. I thought the *hospitalero* didn't speak English, but asked again just to check. He didn't. I took a deep breath and tried *'Hay un hombre en los servicios. No puede salir'.* He leapt to his feet, he obviously knew what I was talking about. He used force on the door, splintering some of the wood around the latch and released the distressed young man.

We met a Canadian woman with a big pack coming the other way. Only a very few people walked the other way. Of course, in the Middle Ages it would have been two-way traffic, with just as many people coming back from Santiago. Apart from the ones who had died en route of course, and there are cemeteries full of them. She was mostly camping, roughing it, hence the big pack. She remarked that she thought she was coming to the best part of the camino, meaning Navarre and the Pyrenees, now behind us. In terms of landscape immediately on the camino, she was right.

It was around now in one of the cafés along the way my attention was drawn to the big TV by the fact that the cafe owner and the locals were listening to a news report with some concern. A pilgrim, a Chinese-American woman called Denise Thiem, had disappeared on a section of the camino ahead of us. She had last been seen in Astorga, and failed to arrive at El Ganso. It's still a complete mystery as I write this. News like this could affect the livelihoods of people who depend on the camino. Considering the huge numbers that walk the camino every year and the slight risks we face every day in our normal lives like road traffic, this shouldn't logically put anybody off, but people tend to over-react to what's in the news. There's far more going on in the world than there is in the news.

We set off towards Logroño. We stopped for lunch at Viana, where there was a bit of a do going on. The streets were filled with people, even more so when the crowds emerged from the big church after the Sunday morning mass. It was the finishing point of a marathon. We overheard pilgrims on a nearby table talking about a terrible snorer in the dorm at Sansol the night before. We set off as the first runners came in. We were allowed to walk down the course (the marathon route followed the camino at least at this point, but in the opposite direction) despite the crowds being kept out of the way behind tapes by marshals. Maybe we pilgrims were part of the show in our distinctive attire. We were trusted to use our common sense and not interfere with the race. We're never trusted to use common-sense at home. I warned Rachel to keep well clear of a blind corner - I once ran a marathon a long time ago, and knew the runners would take a 'racing line' even around a blind corner, and indeed they did.

The city of Logroño was hidden from us by an unusually shaped flat-topped hill until we skirted the sides of the hill and saw both the city and the Rio Ebro. I felt we were now deeply into Spain. I expected us to reach Pamplona at least, whatever happened. I thought that if we reached Logroño we had a good chance of making it all the way to Santiago. The Ebro is a river I've always known about, from staring at maps. It's the river that gives Iberia its name. After wandering around a bit, we settled on the albergue Santiago Apostol, where we expected to see Mary-Ellen again.

The *hospitalero* spoke only Spanish. I wanted to ask questions about smaller rooms, but my Spanish wasn't good enough. If I used the word *habitacion* he thought I was asking about private rooms. There were leaflets about other albergues further along the camino detailing the options available at each one, but no information displayed about the options at the one I was checking into. He didn't seem to expect me to ask any questions, he seemed to expect me to take what he was giving us, which was two beds in the big dorm, so we did.

We ate in the cavernous, wonderfully old-fashioned and ironically named Café Moderno, packed with a mixture of locals playing cards and pilgrims having their *menu peregrino*. Around 10pm we went back to the albergue and went to bed.

The dormitory was reminiscent of Roncesvalles, a historic building but modern on the inside. The bunks were organised by partitions into cubicles of 4 beds. We were in one in the corner with Mary-Ellen, with a Spanish couple on the other side of the partition. There was a block of showers and toilets, and on the far side of that, another dorm just like ours. All this was under a very high vaulted wooden ceiling, effectively one huge dorm as the partitions only went just high enough for privacy. I lay there waiting for sleep. The usual snoring started, especially the Spanish man just the other side of the partition, nothing serious. I had my ear-plugs in. For me, the ear-plugs don't keep out all the noise but they do take the edge off it enough to fall asleep. I always travel with ear-plugs, not just on the camino - if it's not snorers, which are a phenomenon on the camino, it's something else - mopeds (the bane of the Mediterranean lands), barking dogs or disco bars (not a problem on the camino). The symphony developed, the snorers subconsciously synchronising to each others rhythms.

Then it began. When he started, all other snorers immediately fell silent, as if out of respect for the master of snoring. I suppose they'd all been woken, every one. He must have been big, lots of penetrating bass, but a surprisingly fast rhythm, and relentless. Except not quite. The brain has a chance of getting used to a relentless rhythm, screening it out as 'normal'. He would stop now and again, unpredictably. Whenever you dared to hope he had stopped for good it would start again. It didn't seem human.

I lay there for a couple of hours, it seemed even longer, then decided to get up and walk around. I worked out he was in the dorm on the other side of the toilet block. It was actually slightly quieter inside the toilet block, even though that was closer to him, because it had proper walls. The sound was bouncing off the high sloping ceilings from one dorm to the other. I went out of the door on the other side of the toilet block and worked out which bunk was his. It was too dark to see his face. I just had an impression of a tall man in a black sleeping bag. I wanted to know who it was so I could avoid him in future. I considered waking him, but wasn't brave enough, besides, that should really be done by someone lying closer to him. It could have been Australian John, I don't know. The evidence suggests it was.

Having worked out where he was, I moved my bedding to the furthest corner of our dorm. There were plenty of empty spaces. I passed another couple of hours here, but it made no difference. I returned to where Rachel was, where I had started. It was about 2:30am by then. If I had been on my own I would have packed my bags and gone out into the night and started walking out of the city, if I could have got out of the albergue. I did fall asleep. Apparently, whoever it was had got up very early and gone, perhaps not wanting to face anybody in the morning. Or maybe he'd been woken by someone and decided to leave.

You shouldn't really be angry with anyone for snoring, because they can't help it. Nevertheless, it seems so unfair that out of between 50 and 100 people in the albergue, the only one who slept was the one who stopped anyone else sleeping. Mary-Ellen said she just tried praying when she couldn't sleep, but then she was a saint, and saw the best in everybody. Of course one should be tolerant. But sleep deprivation is a form of torture.

*

The next morning we helped Mary-Ellen find her way out of the city and do some business in a bank. By the time we reached the outskirts we were sharing the wide path with what seemed like thousands of locals walking their children to school and then returning home the same way. The excellent path continued out of the suburbs through parkland and by a lake. The altered state of consciousness arising from the nearly sleepless night was strangely pleasant, a sort of holiday mood. I didn't have to drive a car or go to work. In didn't matter if I was a bit dozy. The way deteriorated as we walked between two *autopistas* (motorways/freeways) and through a highway construction site. When we reached agricultural land we were reminded we were now in Rioja (we entered Rioja at Logroño). The soil in the vineyards was clearly a deep rich red, much like the wine it produced. They say this turns to heavy clay that sticks to your boots in wet weather, slowing you down, but we had been lucky with the weather. The little rain we had seen hadn't soaked us or the earth yet.

Lunch was *bocadillo de queso (sin jamon* for Rachel, naturally), *zumo de naranja* and *café grande con leche* in the main square in Navarete. The breakfast hadn't amounted to much at the albergue Santiago Apostol. Oddly, the way returned to the autopista for a while. We branched off on the alternative green route to our accommodation at the San Saturnino albergue in Ventosa. The official, main route carried on by the autopista a bit longer.

This was the first of a number of points where the 'green' alternative route was actually the original route but the authorities had 'improved' it by providing a specially made hard path right next to a new main road. These new 'improved' routes were generally a few hundred metres shorter, but give me the 'green' routes any day. It's not a race.

Mary-Ellen turned up at the albergue an hour or so later than us. Her bag had been delivered to the bar at the other end of the village. She was hot and tired, so I went to fetch it for her. When I got there, I said to the barmaid I had come to collect a backpack belonging to an American woman called Mary-Ellen, and she handed it over to me without asking who I was. I can't imagine that happening at home.

In the kitchen we talked to a young Jamaican

woman cooking her tea, the only black person I met to talk to on the camino. She was in good spirits despite having got lost and gone 3 hours off the way that day. She didn't sound Jamaican (I lived in the West Indies for two years a long time ago), but she had moved to New York at a young age.

We shared our dorm with five young Germans, must have been in their early twenties. We were to see them off and on for much of the camino. They seemed happy to spend time with us, despite the age gap and having to speak our language. The young all come equipped with smart-phones, tablets or Kindles, and face a daily search for Wifi and a place to plug in.

By now my camino beard was developing. I had shaved for the last time the day before leaving home. Nowadays the beard comes through white. When I was young, like the five Germans, it came through reddish, despite me having brown hair on my head. I also now looked like I spent every day in the sun. We both opted for long sleeves and long trousers to reduce the area to be covered in sun cream every morning. The trousers and shirts were light and cool, easy to wash and dry. The alternative, which many others adopted, was shorts and T-shirt, but then you have to cover your arms and legs in goo which attracts the dust of the road, deep red in Rioja. The resulting gunge mixes with sweat, gets on your shirt and has to be washed off. There are arguments both ways. Anyway it wasn't high summer, and shorts aren't quite right in some places. We both wore light wide-brimmed hats, like most pilgrims. When I was young I never wore a hat and never had any problems with sun or heatstroke even in the two years I lived and worked in the tropics, but then I had a thick head of hair. They used to call me 'white rasta', but that was a long time ago. I still have a full head of hair, but it's thin enough to get burnt through, so a hat is essential.

*

The next day we walked on through Najera and Azofra, forests and hills to start with then red-earth arable land. We could see snow on high mountains to our south and measure our forward progress from their changing aspects. More disappointingly, we could also see and hear the A-12 *autopista* about a mile away to the north.

The time had come to attempt my first phone call in Spanish. We needed to secure our accommodation in Cirueña. It was a long walk from Azofra, and would be very long day, for us, if we had to go on beyond Cirueña to Santo Domingo. Also, we fancied staying in a private room in a pension. I took out my mobile (cell-phone) and dialled the number from Brierley's book. The lady only spoke Spanish. I managed to book a double room, and answer when I was asked when I expected to arrive. Phew.

It's not the custom to book ahead generally. The municipal albergues don't take advance bookings, but the private ones do and so of course do pensions and hotels. We only called ahead on occasions when we were concerned about finding somewhere, or wanted something special.

Cirueña was the strangest town we saw in Spain. First we came to the golf-course on top of the hill, in the middle of miles and miles of farmland and the only golf-course we saw on our journey. The greens and fairways were obviously looked after, but I could see only one person playing. Then we came to a modern housing estate. With nobody living there. Block after block of modern, empty houses. A major building project gone completely wrong. No other human beings apart from the young Germans who were never far away. After a mile of this we came to the tiny old part of the village. We found our pension, Casa Victoria. Our hosts' family were the only locals we ever saw in this place. Our hosts told us only about a dozen people lived in the village. We had our evening meal at the small albergue, also run by the same people, dining with mostly French speakers. Our hosts' children were doing their homework at the end of the table, probably absorbing other languages at the same time.

*

The next morning we set off across wide open countryside downhill into Santo Domingo. In Santo Domingo, after 200km of walking, we encountered the first public toilet we had seen in Spain. It was locked. It was to be the only public toilet we ever saw in Spain.

It's a beautiful old town. We should have been interested in the cathedral, but dived into a coffee shop instead. We would have had to queue behind a coach party for tickets to the cathedral. It turned out to be a good move. The coffee shop was really a high-class chocolate shop. I come from a long line of chocoholics. We had our coffee with fruit covered in dark chocolate, with a dark chocolate *peregrino* each to finish.

The complete absence of public toilets on a route walked by over a hundred thousand people every year seems odd. In the countryside but near to towns there would often be an *area de descanso* with everything for a picnicking family escaping from the heat of the city - tables and benches, swings for the children, a *fuente* dispensing drinking water - but no toilet. In the towns and villages you are expected to use the cafés, but this involves buying a drink that you may not actually want. The proprietors are quite keen on spotting people just popping in to use the loo. A few, very reasonably, have a sign saying you can use the loo if you pay 50c. Fair enough. But in the vast majority of places you feel morally or practically obliged to sit down and have a drink.

At home, even the smallest public places are obliged to provide toilets. It's a problem for small, old buildings like village halls or churches. But even in the cathedral in Santiago, which generally holds a thousand people, there is no toilet. You have to go outside, cross the square to one of the touristy cafés and buy a pointless coffee.

After Santo Domingo the way was less pleasant, being alongside the N-120, a *nacional* route, the equivalent of an A road at home, but not all the time. It diverted up to the hilltop village of Grañon and then at the end of our day's walk to the village of Viloria de la Rioja.

My camera mysteriously stopped working at a café in Grañon, where we sat in the sun and had a coffee with a French cyclist. Yes, you can bike the camino, that would make you a *bicigrino*. Numerous attempts to revive the camera failed, including changing the battery. It was a 12-year old compact, only very simple. I never let photography dominate any travel, especially this trip. My photos are snaps to bring back memories of people and places, not works of art. There's something disrespectful about grabbing lots of photos of strange places. You could say unspiritual - trying to capture the moment and store it, instead of being in the moment and experiencing it fully. But I was a bit sad. I though I might buy a replacement when we got to Burgos, but that might not work. Most people buy from the internet nowadays, not an option for me on the camino. When I got over it, it dawned on me I had a camera on my antiquated (also 12 years old) mobile phone. This wasn't ideal, there was a blemish on the lens that appeared on every shot and the quality wasn't great, but at least I'd get something. My friends loved the photos because what we were seeing and doing was so interesting. Who cares about the technical quality.

At Viloria we stayed at Acacio y Orietta, now one my favourite albergues, named after the two *hospitaleros* Acacio from Brazil and his partner Orietta from Italy. We actually got off on the wrong foot. We had expected it to be a vegetarian albergue, as it was marked with a V in the guide-book. This turned out to be a simple mistake in the book, one the *hospitaleros* had not been aware of until that moment, even though they knew John Brierley personally. We were travelling with the latest edition which had only been published three months before we set off. Acacio said they didn't do vegetarian food because they wanted to be open to all spiritual traditions. This didn't make sense to me. That's an argument for vegetarianism, not against it, as then you could accommodate Buddhists, Hindus, Jews, Muslims whatever. But these were good people and I didn't want to argue.

The food was excellent. The main dish was a thick lentil broth *lentejas* with *chorizo* added for flavour, great for me. The first course was a thick tasty vegetable soup. This combined with a locally grown cauliflower that Orietta had rustled up and the rice we all had, made a good veggie meal for Rachel by pouring the thick soup over the rice and cauliflower. Everybody was happy.

We dined with two cyclists from Brazil and a young man from Hungary. The cyclists also spoke English, but naturally were enjoying the opportunity to speak Portuguese. Acacio spoke Portuguese with them, English with us, and Italian with his wife. The young Hungarian was left out a bit. He spoke some German, but very little English, Spanish or any other language. He was limping badly. We managed to communicate a bit. He was walking 40km a day. He said his leg hurt at the end of the day but was always alright in the morning. I don't know if he made it all the way. I would say he wouldn't, he was trying to do too much each day, there was a long way to go and he was falling apart already. One other pilgrim turned up, but had to leave as she couldn't tolerate the incense that pervaded the albergue. I quite liked it, but she couldn't help it, she had a physical reaction to it.

So there were only 5 of us in a dorm (the only dorm) that would not have been crowded even if all 10 beds were taken. Some were bunks, some were freestanding. The albergue was warm and cosy. It was cold outside at night at that elevation. Possibly the most comfortable and peaceful night of the whole camino.

Acacio is the god-father of the famous Brazilian author, Paulo Coelho. Paulo Coelho walked the camino in 1986. He experienced some kind of transformation on the way, writing the novel *Pilgrimage* on his return and his most famous novel *The Alchemist* the following year. He has become the best-selling writer in the Portuguese language. He is the patron of this albergue, and his latest writings were on sale there.

*

We had crossed from Rioja to Castilla the day we arrived at Acacio y Orietta, but ahead of us now in the distance we could see a more physical border, the mountains marking the near edge of the *meseta*, the high table-land that bears the middle third of the camino. I say mountains, we could see high mountains still sporting snowfields away to the south, but the mountains ahead of us were more like high rounded hills covered in green forest. These lay between us and Burgos, now three days walk away.

In the heyday of the camino in the Middle Ages most of the pilgrims, and the knights, tradesmen, monks etc that came with them, came from France. They were encouraged to stay and settle in the lands only recently reconquered from the Moors, lands depopulated from centuries of war and instability. These masses would help in repopulating and re-Christianising northern Spain. They founded many Villafrancas along or near the way. That night's destination was Villafranca Montes de Oca, the last village before the empty 'mountains'.

The municipal albergue was bang on the busy N-120, with lorries thundering past the open dormitory windows, so we went instead to the San Anton

Abad, a hotel but with a pilgrim albergue built on the side, set well away from the road. We dined and had breakfast in unaccustomed elegance in the hotel dining room, which nevertheless offered a good-value 'pilgrim menu'. In the dorm we met again the three over-seventies Americans we had met at Orisson and last seen when we had passed them the following morning in the fog, climbing up to the Col de Lepoeder, 12 days ago. Nancy was losing a toenail, but otherwise they were getting on fine.

The dorm was full but spacious, and unusually dark. In fact, it was pitch black when Nancy turned out the light at 10pm. I had a lightweight torch in the bottom of my pack, but I'd never needed it on the trip so far. Most dorms had over-bright emergency lights telling you, if you couldn't work it out, where the *salida* (exit) was. It was invariably out of the door you had just come in by. I had already memorised the layout, including the fact that my bed was the third one away from the door in case I needed to go to the loo in the night, as proved to be the case after all the wine and water with the generous pilgrim meal. Even so, I walked into the cupboard next to the door on my first attempt. I knew the return journey would be even trickier, partly because the bright automatic lights in the loo would destroy my night-vision. Actually, it was completely black in the dorm anyway. I steered from the foot of one bed to the next, counting beds, and found the right one to get into. Wouldn't want any misunderstandings or international incidents at that time of night.

*

Rachel woke me in the morning. It was still dark, but I managed to put on the clothes I'd put by the side of the bed, pick up my wash-kit and head to the bathroom. There I looked at my watch. It was 5:30, not 6:30. No wonder no-one else had got up. Rachel had mistaken the time. She'd been panicked by some very early risers into thinking it was later than it was. We couldn't do anything without disturbing people who were still sleeping, so we just had to wait out the odd hour.

When I say early-risers, these people must have got up about 4:30. Sunrise isn't till 7am. We encountered people like this along the camino. They would get up in the dark with their head-torches and carry their backpacks and sleeping bags out of the dorms to carry on packing outside, to minimise the disturbance to the rest of us. But flashing head-torches and rustling bags are disturbing. Some people's head-torches are like demented light-houses as they move around, up and down, flashing their beams into every corner of the dorm. Why do they do it? Probably because some guide-book tells them to. In the summer, you do have to avoid the heat, and I can see the point of being on the road as early as sunrise. It usually took us till 8am or more to get going, but I can see why people leave at 7am. But 5am? It's dark outside, very dark, there is not much twilight before the dawn. They have to walk for at least the first hour with good torches. By roads, or on rough ground, that's dangerous. And you miss seeing stuff. And, I feel, you should really try to fit in with what everyone else is doing, so that we all get enough sleep. Ah, the tension between modern individualists thrust into an older, communal way of life.

We stayed for the magnificent breakfast and set off earlier than usual up the track through the woods. There would be nowhere else to eat or drink for 12km. The walk continued through deep pine forests, far enough from the N-120, a contrast to the previous couple of days.

We came to an eerie monument to the fallen, the *monumento de los caìdos*. What struck me from a distance was that on this most religious of walks, in a catholic country where every grave or memorial I had seen was adorned with a cross, on this monument in a place where hundreds of people died there was not a single cross to be seen. I knew why. The 'fallen' were in fact massacred prisoners on the losing side in the Spanish Civil War, between Republicans and Nationalists. The Republicans were a coalition of workers parties, socialists, communists and anarchists. Not a lot in common with the Republican party in the States. The Nationalists were a coalition of royalists, fascists and conservatives. The Catholic church at the time sided explicitly with the Nationalists, the side which did this massacre. Hence the lack of catholic symbols. That wouldn't seem appropriate to the relatives of those who were killed. The monument couldn't even be built until nearly 40 years later, when Franco died. Of course, there were massacres on both sides.

Just as the Second World War is still embedded in the minds of people from those countries that took part in it, even though they mostly weren't born at the time, so the echoes of the Spanish Civil War still shape people's perspectives today. At least the Second World War ended in 1945. Franco held on until 1975. Hence graffiti along the way like *ni dioses ni reyes* - 'no gods or kings'.

Glorious walking through miles of heather and pine forests, then a gradual descent to villages. We had thought to stop at Agès as the guide-book indicated small dorms and a veggie menu at one of the albergues there, but when we got there it was locked, the menu looked far from veggie and we could see the beds in the dorms were touching, so we pressed on to Atapuerca.

I'd heard of Atapuerca, a place where the remains of our earliest ancestors *homo antecessor* were found. I'm not sure if they're actually direct ancestors or more like distant uncles. Very distant. If I understand the latest theories the ancestors of anybody able to read this were in Africa before 60,000 years ago, although I suspect I may have more Neanderthal than most. The actual *Parque Arqueologico* was 3km off route. The subject does interest me, but I could see the site was attended by tourist coaches and I didn't feel the urge to look round a visitor centre.

*

We'd crossed the mountains that defined the border of the *meseta* but had not yet sighted Burgos, there was just one isolated hill in the way. In the cool, grey morning the next day we climbed steadily up and saw to the west Burgos and the plains beyond. It was British weather - low grey skies and a cold wind but no rain. The landscape was a deep green all around. We could just see the spires of the cathedral far away.

We successfully negotiated Brierley's alternative *opcion* navigating every twist left and right on the countryside earth tracks, emerging on the main route at the village of Orbaneja, much to the surprise of the two Dutch brothers who had left us behind and then found us just in front of them. We had the privilege of having that peaceful section of the walk to ourselves, with views across the fields to Burgos.

The route necessarily became more urban, crossing the bypasses, skirting the airport. We took another 'green' alternative into town along the riverbank. The walks into city always seem to be longer than you expect. It was a pleasant route, and we were lucky with the cool weather, but it was the end of the day, and I couldn't help feeling inferior to all the fresh-looking locals in the park. They seemed to respect what we were doing, greeting us with a genial 'Buen Camino'. We met the five young Germans again. They tended to walk at different speeds, then stop and wait for each other, which was often when we would spot them.

We picked a bridge over the river and entered the old city of Burgos.

THE SECOND BIT - LA MESETA

We landed on our feet in Burgos. We walked down the old street following the brass scallop shells set into the pavement, as they had been in Pamplona, and flanked by handsome historic buildings. We came to a four-star hotel, the Palacio Blasones, offering special rates for pilgrims. We thought even the special rate would be out of our league, but we were offered a room for only €60 a night. You couldn't get a simple bed and breakfast for that at home.

The room was on the top floor. We unlocked the door and were surprised to see only a staircase that led up to what was obviously an attic room under the sloping roof, but spacious. I looked around. I reckoned you could get at least 20 bunk beds in there. It didn't seem right to have all that space to ourselves. There were two big double-beds, and both a bath and a shower. Rachel disappeared into the bathroom for a very long time. I heard lots of splashing, and contented sighs. Soon it looked like Crocodile Dundee's New York hotel bedroom, with lines of washing strung between the rafters.

The next day we walked further down the street to the cathedral, passing the albergue where we knew the young Germans were staying. I must admit, it did look more interesting in there. Lots of young people, coming and going. Behind its 16th century façade were 4 floors with beds for 150 pilgrims.

We did the audio tour of the cathedral. The cathedral contains 21 individual chapels, each a work of art, in fact each containing many historic works of art. The audio guide recited the names and dates of the artists and patrons of each - too much information, for us. Better to soak up the atmosphere of the whole. Pride of place is given to the tomb of El Cid and his wife. El Cid was far from being a religious man himself, not exactly one to 'turn the other cheek'. He was very much the medieval warlord, and a very intelligent and successful one at that. He is thought of as a Castilian, Spanish and Christian hero who fought against the Moors, partly because of the classic Hollywood movie 'El Cid', where he was played by Charlton Heston. The film rather simplified the story. At times in his 'career' he actually fought for Muslim masters against Christians, sometimes the other way round, but always really just for himself. 'El Cid' is actually a Moorish term of respect.

He lived and died in the 11th century, and was originally buried elsewhere with his beloved war-horse, Babieco, as he had requested. It wasn't until the 20th century (1919) that his body was dug up and re-interred more conventionally alongside his wife in the cathedral.

The cathedral wasn't built until the 13th century,

the heyday of the camino, when there was a flood of French culture into northern Spain - warriors, craftsmen, artists, merchants. It's almost entirely Gothic, only a few later Renaissance embellishments, including the striking Golden Staircase. The old cities on the camino are heavily medieval. I get the impression that not only the industrial revolution but also the renaissance passed them by, which is what makes them special. From the 12th until the 14th century they were where it was all happening, they had the wealth to fund great buildings and attract the best artists in Europe. Since then, history has happened somewhere else, and you can still feel the spirit of that time. It's true of many of the churches along the way too. It's part of the essence of the camino.

We decided to be retro and send some postcards, something I haven't done for a while. The Post Office was more challenging than I thought. Even in this town, they weren't expecting foreigners. You couldn't go to a desk, show your post-cards and deliver the practised line '*seis sellos por Inglaterra, por favor*'. It wasn't that simple. You first had to take a ticket to join a queue, fair enough, but there were several queues and you had to work out which queue would be the one that sold stamps. I didn't see the word *sellos* anywhere. I stood there conspicuously clutching the post-cards and peering at the signs in Spanish, hoping someone would point me to the right queue. They did.

In the city we had a break from the 'pilgrim

menus'. It proved harder to find veggie options, probably because it was harder to discuss it with busy bar staff than with *hospitaleros* well used to foreigners and their ways. Dining just the two of us in the small bars and cafés around the Plaza Mayor was such a change. Like being on holiday. There was a girl in one of the cafés who spoke fluent English because she had done much the same work in a pub in London for a few years. Apart from her, no-one else we spoke to spoke English. Burgos was not a cosmopolitan city. We pilgrims were the colourful but strange minority.

*

We walked out of Burgos in the company of our new friend Pia, originally from Italy but married to a German and living in Germany. All did not seem to be going well on that front. She was catholic, and passionate about the medieval, even resenting the renaissance decorations on top of the gothic cathedral. This was something she'd been burning to do for a long time, and had finally been released by her husband and children to go and do it. She was younger and fitter than us and went on ahead.

We walked at first through pleasant countryside, and then got caught up in diversions around motorway construction sites before coming to the village of Tardajos, which could be said to be the start of the meseta proper. A flat-topped hill clearly indicated our direction ahead. We stopped for a drink and rest in Rabé, where the very friendly barman gave me a token I carried all the way to Santiago, before tackling the 8km up and over the bare and empty hill to our destination that night, Hornillos del Camino. Rachel was hesitant to stay there because she had read on the internet it was 'bed-bug city' at some point in the past. But as they say when selling stocks and shares, past history is no guide to future performance. We picked the most modern albergue (Meeting Point) and had no problems.

We dined at a table with the two Dutch brothers, Peter and Harry. We talked about the group of Scotsmen wearing kilts that had passed us that afternoon. They were very amused when I told them it was forbidden to wear anything at all under the kilt, even on a windy day. There was only one tiny bar in which to eat, everyone had to squeeze in and share tables. As soon as we were finished, we had to leave the table. Others were standing waiting. Everybody got fed in the end.

*

The next day was our first day entirely on the meseta. We began to get the feel of the landscape. These flat-topped hills were a striking feature. The meseta seemed to exist on two levels, a little over 100m apart vertically, flat on top, flat down below with relatively steep climbs up or down between the two. At that time of year everything was green. Fifty shades of green. There were noticeably fewer trees, and no vineyards any more, only arable fields growing cereals. Some bits of land on the steep hills-sides looked drier, more Mediterranean. But it was colder, partly because this flat land is surprisingly high (800 to 900 metres) and partly because the wind was now blowing from the north. I'm told that in summer everything is brown and the meseta turns into an oven, but that wasn't our experience, far from it.

At the end of this our second day on the meseta we came to Castrojeriz, a picturesque village at the foot of one these hills with a ruined castle on the top. Again we stayed in a very modern albergue, called Ultreia like the one in Saint Jean. We went for our showers. The symbols on the doors of the showers were a bit 'arty'. It wasn't obvious at first glance which was which - men's or women's. Something like a scallop shell for the ladies and a pilgrim staff and gourd for the men. I'd just emerged from my shower, without even a towel, when a woman walked in and looked around. Luckily, she was German so it didn't matter.

We got our washing on the line in the sun, ahead of our usual schedule. We could have climbed the hill to look at the castle, or looked round this quite large and interesting village, but we didn't. The garden at the back was very pleasant, and we just stayed there, all afternoon, watching the world go by and chatting mostly to two sisters from Holland. They were lean and fit, and quite focused and organised, but not as laid back as most pilgrims. They finished early every day, before midday, having walked generally without stopping. They also started early, which was a bit of a problem for the rest of us.

There was a communal meal in the evening, one of the reasons we picked this albergue. This was a time of year when you could pick your albergues, in the summer it's 'any port in a storm'. There was a Polish man called Jerzy from Gdynia who was greatly surprised when I sat down next to him and said *dzien dobry*. I had worked as a walking leader in the Tatra mountains in Poland for three months a long time ago. That's about as far as my Polish goes these days. He spoke neither English nor Spanish, but seemed in good spirits. There was Christine from California, another person we were to see a lot of, off and on, all the way to Santiago. There were three Germans opposite me that I hadn't met before, except briefly in the shower, and a young man from Brazil called Jonathan. The Dutch sisters got their own dinner.

Jonathan was the fastest man on the camino. He was skinny and light, with swarthy skin and a goatee beard. He had run all the way from Puy in France, over 1000 km already. He was doing over 40km every day. Yes, he was running a cross-country marathon every day. I did run a marathon once, when I was young. I didn't feel like getting up the next day and doing it again. He was the least tired person I met on the camino, full of energy. He earned his supper by acting as an interpreter between our *hospitalero*, who spoke only Spanish, and the rest of us round the table.

The albergue had been a bodega in the old days. In fact, there was a wine press taking up much of the dining room. The *hospitalero* gave a talk after dinner, explaining how the wine press worked, Jonathan interpreting all the time. Then we went down into the old cellars for more history. All the time Jonathan was interpreting fluently, without even thinking, between Spanish and English. Neither was his own language - he was from Brazil, so he spoke Portuguese.

We went to bed early, about 9pm, and were surprised to find the lights out and the two Dutch sisters asleep. We got ready for bed as quietly as we could and got into our bunks. After half an hour, the Germans came in, talking loudly and put the lights on. I heard what sounded like swearing in Dutch. The Germans went to bed and the lights went off again about 10pm, as normal.

*

The idea was in this albergue that we would be woken gradually by the sound of Gregorian chanting about 6:30. A nice touch, like at Roncevalles. However, this didn't fit with the Dutch women's self-imposed schedule, so we were woken by flickering head-torches at about 5:30. I couldn't really hear the Gregorian changing for the sounds of gear being stuffed into rucksacks and plastic bags being rustled. Maybe nobody told them.

People have different ways of doing the camino, and that's fair enough. But the albergues are part of what we come to experience. Many have an ethos, it seems disrespectful to ignore it even if it's not the ethos we practise in our daily life in the 'real world'.

The albergues could be quite different from each other. They're not part of a chain. They can be quite offbeat and idiosyncratic, like Acacio and Orieta. Some are Christian, some are rooted more in Eastern religion. Some are run by local government, some are private businesses. Some are just the village pub. They're all interesting in their different ways. We'd experienced some of each by now.

We set off up the last of the flat-topped hills, pausing on the top to look back at Castrojeriz. As we contemplated the steep descent in front of us, Jonathan ran up to us. I had thought he would have been well in front of us by now, but he had had to run back to the albergue for his camera. He hadn't found it there, so he decided to look for it in the last place he took a photo. This was in the ruined castle on top of the hill, but that didn't bother him. He liked running up and down hills. He did find his camera there, ran back down the hill, across the plain and up the one we were standing on, pausing only briefly to chat to us. I wondered how he would tackle the steep descent. He ran down in tight zig-zags, seeming to float down to the bottom, then ran off into the distance. We never saw him again.

The countryside ahead was flatter, with fewer and lower hills. The mountains were receding further into the distance to the south and to the north. Everything in front of us was green. You could say the landscape was getting duller, many have written that about the meseta, but I never got bored on this or any section of the walk. There was always something to measure your progress by.

We had thought to stay at Boadilla, where there was an albergue run by an artist and his family. We heard later from the Dutch brothers, always a good judge of places to stay, they had good food and a warm welcome there. We decided to press on a bit further to Fromista. I knew this to be the southernmost point of the camino, a turning point on the picture of the path I had in my mind. We walked along a canal, common in the lowlands at home but a rarity on the camino. There were locks, but the sturdy steel gates that would have been needed to control the water were missing, so the water poured freely down man-made waterfalls.

At Fromista we stayed in an albergue converted from railway station buildings, on the platform. The station and the railway were still functioning, in fact we passed through Fromista at speed on our way home at the end of the trip. We took a private room with shower here, and so did Kate and Kelsey. They were both from the States, almost half a century apart in age, and both were artists. Kelsey was walking the camino as part of her college degree. Kate was retired. Both kept notebooks full of sketches. In fact, they both asked if they could sketch my feet. I've never had two women sketching my bare feet before. They travelled well together, looking out for each other. Kelsey was young and beautiful. Kate was an experienced traveller (she had recently worked for Peace Corps in Africa) and older than us.

There was only one other pilgrim staying there, a Polish man who had been stuck there for several days with serious problems. He had planned to do the whole camino walking 35 km a day, but his knees had got worse and worse, and he had ground to a complete halt here in Fromista. He was too crippled even to give up and catch a bus or train. He couldn't walk across the room without a stick, and without holding on to furniture. His knees had swollen to the size of melons. To add to his problems he could speak neither English nor Spanish. One of the reasons he had chosen this place to break down was that the *hospitalera* was Russian. I didn't find out how she came to be running an albergue in rural Spain, she could only speak Spanish to me. I know the Poles don't like to admit it, but if they're desperate, they can talk to Russians. He wasn't our age, he was only in his thirties. He used his smartphone to show pictures of his knees to his doctor in Poland. They sure looked bad to me.

*

Brierley's guide-book warned us of the 'soulless

senda' the next day, the hard path made for pilgrims alongside the relentlessly straight main road for miles and miles. We opted for Brierley's 'green' route on a path along a river for most of the way. It seemed a no-brainer to us, it was only 900m longer but it surprised us how few people took it. We met a Spanish man selling almonds along the way. As far as I could understand him (not very far) the river route was the original route, but the *politicos* had moved the official route to the road to go past their mates' cafés.

We saw a tall figure in the distance, looking back towards us. As we approached, we could hear him singing, and see he was wearing a tabard with 'Are we nearly there yet?' written on it in big letters. This turned out to be John from Australia, not the notorious snorer we had encountered earlier. This was a charismatic if eccentric man with a twinkle in his eye, tall, bearded and 78 years old. We quickly received his life history. He'd been born in India, gone to school in England and emigrated to Australia. Whenever England played Australia at cricket, he supported England, so he said, just to wind his mates up. He thought this would be his last camino. As we parted, he told us to see God in everyone we met.

We walked into Carrion de los Condes and lodged at the Santa Clara convent. We didn't see any nuns, at least I didn't. One man ran the albergue part, and the attached museum. The nuns kept out of sight. The building we stayed in was from the thirteenth century. We had a small room with just two small beds, the stone walls completely bare apart from a crucifix. Saint Francis of Assisi had stayed in this very building, eight centuries before us. It was only 7 euros a night each.

The museum contained nativity scenes sent to the convent from all over the world. The next morning Rachel did see a nun, by accident when she went back for something. The nuns did the cleaning, while the man dealt with the passing heathens.

*

The next day was the longest stretch of the camino without a café, village or any facilities of any kind. It was also one of only two days when the weather was less than pleasant. This stretch was only 17km and flat, not so daunting, it just meant it was a good idea to carry a packed lunch, and enough water. The wind was in our faces and quite strong, the strongest wind we encountered in Spain, like a brisk day in the Lake District. The showers were light. Enough to make us keep our waterproofs on, not enough for the rain to get inside the pack. We covered the distance quickly, for us. There was nowhere sheltered to linger.

Eventually we came to Calzadilla about lunch-time and went straight to the hotel-albergue Camino Real. There was a huge mound of backpacks and another of boots in the entrance. Beyond this we reached the crowds of pilgrims, some huddled round tables with their coffees and teas, the rest still waiting at the bar. There were about four or five people behind the bar, each trying to serve several people as fast as they could, mostly with hot drinks. I waited alongside John, the tall Australian/Brit we'd met the previous day. He was drinking a stiff glass of the local fire-water. I asked him how it was going. He confessed he'd accepted a lift to there, where he was staying the night. He said he'd been offered a lift by a man in a car called Jesus, so he felt he couldn't refuse.

There was no rush for us. We'd done most of the day's walk and waited patiently for our *cafés grandes con leche*. The crowds thinned out as people moved on, we got served and found a space at a table with about 10 other people, conversing mostly in English.

Rested and warmed, we went on towards Ledigos. For once, we didn't take the green alternative. I saw the stone marker, but the path leading across fields into woods had no boot-prints, and I wasn't sure. As it turned out, this bit of *senda* wasn't too bad, and we did meet a small Danish girl with a big pack who caught up with us. She was doing 40 km a day, mostly camping wild, sometimes staying in an albergue for a shower and relative comfort. She put us to shame, we thought we were roughing it in the albergues, checking into pensions now and again for a break.

We stayed in the albergue in Ledigos, the Danish

girl went ahead. This was also the village bar, and like many such places the front door was wide open to the elements, to encourage people in. Why anyone would want to come in when it was just as cold inside as it was outside I don't know. The albergue boasted a courtyard and even a small swimming pool, but neither was much use in the cold wind. They did have the heating on in the dormitory, which was where all the pilgrims were congregated, gazing at their phones and tablets as the room was far too dark and gloomy to read a book.

Despite the fact that I had worked my whole life in computers, writing software from a time before people even had digital watches up until almost now, I was the only person on the camino not actually carrying one. Maybe that's why I wasn't carrying one. I can see the point. Keeping the weight down is critical. I was carrying a guide-book (actually two, Brierley's latest, plus one I'd bought earlier that just had the maps), a camera (now deceased) and mobile phone, plus spare batteries for the camera (now useless) and a charger for the phone. All these functions could be combined in one contemporary device, with a single charger.

But I decided not to go out and buy a shiny new device just before the camino. For one thing, no-one ever steals my gadgets for the same reasons no-one ever steals my clothes - they're old, tatty and deeply unfashionable - so I never have to worry about them. And for another, I'd have to learn how to use it while on the camino. People might see me trying to work it out, getting cross and having to ask a young person. They might laugh. Besides, I know what I'm like. I'm an information addict, an internet junky, I'd be burying myself in my smart-phone when I should be opening my mind and experiencing the world immediately around me, the camino, the pilgrims.

It would have been useful though - weather forecasts, research about cities ahead of us, making travel arrangements etc. You could keep in touch with friends and family too, though I don't quite see why everyone should have to. People seem to call out the Guardia Civil, or at least go on Facebook, if they haven't heard from someone for a few days. Gone are the days when I would disappear for weeks or even months into the Himalayas or even Scotland without anyone (except my Mum of course) worrying about me.

The weather wasn't conducive to drying clothes outside, so space on the radiators in the dorm was much sought after. People were very fair about sharing it.

I was on a bottom bunk and Rachel was on the top, as usual. The other side of a partition was a young Vietnamese man who didn't speak much English. Only a few days before I'd been listening to Mike's hair raising accounts of being a young soldier in the Vietnam war. Now I'm sleeping next to a very polite young man from Vietnam.

Rachel spotted what looked like a small dark brown beetle crawling up the partition away from her sleeping bag, shortly after we had deployed our bug-repelling bedding. She asked me if I thought it might be a bed-bug. I thought not, on the grounds it was too big, about 4-5 mm, but after reading about it I'm not so sure now. I don't kill insects unnecessarily, but as it's a public health issue I squashed it to make sure. We didn't get any bites and didn't see any at the next place, so if they were there they didn't follow us.

To be fair to the bar, the evening meal was generous in a warm dining room, where we again shared a table with the two brothers, Peter and Harry, from Holland.

*

We took the green route out of Ledigos the next morning, missing out Terradillos de los Templarios, and again after San Nicolas, where the green route across the countryside is actually the old route. This second green route goes away from the lovely N-120, now joined by the A-231 *autopista*, and instead ascends a gentle hill through farmland with views from the top. Most people stuck to the *senda* next to the N-120, one lady seeming quite convinced we'd gone the wrong way.

At some point on today's walk we reached the half-way point on our journey to Santiago. Opinions vary as to exactly where, but there is a rather grand gateway shortly before Sahagun that claims to be the spot. You can get a certificate in Sahagun to celebrate getting half-way, but I thought that would be bad luck.

Sahagun had a bewildering choice of places to stay, at least compared to what we were used to. We bumped into James, whom we'd first met in the crowded little bar in Hornillos del Camino, our first night on the meseta five nights ago. James was a young, bearded, manically extroverted Australian. We were surprised to find out later he was actually a priest. He was enthusiastic about the place where he was staying, the Hotel Alfonso. He was enthusiastic about most things, but this turned out to be a good recommendation.

We checked into our double room, showered and went out to explore. One church was filled with wooden floats bearing statues of Mary, Jesus and saints. We'd seen statues like these carried through the streets by strong men during *semana santa* (holy week) in La Palma in the Canaries, accompanied by brass bands playing mournful Spanish music. It wasn't just a museum, it was where they kept these things ready to be brought out at Easter.

I don't normally comment on art, but what struck me about the medieval art in the old churches, these more recent statues and the modern secular sculptures we saw on the streets of the cities was the intensity of expression in the faces. Pia, herself an

Italian catholic, commented on the Spanish taste for depictions of the agonised Mary holding the dead or dying Jesus. Strong stuff.

We moved on to the Plaza Mayor in search of food and stumbled upon our American friends Jim, Nancy and Bentner that we'd originally met at Orisson and last seen nine days previously at Villafranca Montes de Oca. They'd had some problems with legs and taken the bus for a few stages, hence jumping in front of us, but otherwise they were fine, making steady progress towards Santiago. We had a drink with them, then moved on to find food, actually pizzas, round the corner. Pizzas made a change from the pilgrim menus, provided veggie choices for Rachel and were of good quality throughout Spain. The pizza-place was full of Spanish families. Children were playing football in the street, their dads watching a match on the big TVs that were in all the cafés, their mums chatting in Spanish that was way too fast for me. The street was still lively, in fact getting more so, when we went back to our hotel to bed at 10pm.

*

The weather forecast was rain for the next two days so unusually for us we opted for the dull road route instead of the green route via Calzadilla. I anticipated that the 'natural earth tracks' would turn to mud, and that this would slow Rachel down. Rachel tries to remain clean walking through mud, whereas I think, that's what boots are for. Anyway, no-one can avoid accumulating balls of mud on their boots and that slows you down even if you accept it.

The first of these two days was as wet as promised, our only really wet day on the camino. The waterproofs were thoroughly tested. The rain penetrated the pack, as expected. I had a proper 'storm-proof' liner inside the pack, not just a bin-liner, that no doubt added to the weight of my pack but kept all my gear dry that day.

The two routes diverged at a complex road junction. The routes to Calzada or El Burgo Ranero were clearly marked in big letters painted on the roads in several places. We found our road, to El Burgo Ranero, and were surprised to meet several groups of people coming back the other way. They had intended to take the green route to Calzado, but had missed the turning. Again, the green route used to be the main route. It's always easier to miss signs in bad weather.

One good thing about the new roads that have been built is that the old roads, like the one we were on, are now almost devoid of traffic. We trudged on in the rain, without taking any photos. We stopped for the night at the albergue La Laguna in El Burgo Ranero. It was more like a holiday camp, with wooden chalets, and run by an Italian. It was named after the artificial lake next to the albergue, teeming with wildlife including loud-croaking heavy metal frogs. Probably very pleasant on a sunny day. The

Italian *hospitalero* seemed to like me because I tried to speak Spanish, I had the right change when it came to paying, and I seemed to have the knack of closing the dormitory door. Other people in the queue couldn't speak a work of Spanish, didn't have change and when they closed the dorm door it came open again, so he had to cross the courtyard and shut it properly.

The village was very quiet, what made it for us was the café El Camino. We'd stopped there for a drink on the way in and met the host Manuel from Barcelona (really) and his partner Svetlana from Bulgaria. They had met each other on the camino a few years before. Now they were running a café together, serving passing pilgrims. There were posters about yoga and meditation. They understood vegetarian food. We booked in for the evening meal.

It was like a communal meal in an albergue. Everyone sat down to eat together at one table, at the same time. On my right was sat Christine from California. She enquired whether the lentil dish had chorizo sausage, as she didn't want to eat pork. I asked her if she was vegetarian, and was surprised to learn she was a Muslim, one of only two I met on the camino. She was married to a Saudi man she had met at college, and who was on the phone to her at one point during the meal. I was surprised because as she was telling me this, she had a glass of red wine in her hand and was obviously enjoying it.

There was a German lady opposite me and the two Dutch brothers, again, to my left. Next to Rachel was a Korean man, Dee-Jay, who spoke very good English, and his wife Sunny. Sunny was a very petite lady who had run 80 marathons in different countries. At the end of this memorable and convivial evening Manuel spoke to us all, saying we should take this spirit of international friendship with us back to the countries we came from. Preaching to the already converted really. Disappointingly, four days later there was a General Election in the UK in which UKIP shot to 12 per cent of the vote on an anti-European and anti-immigration platform. To take the wind out of their sails the ruling Conservative party promised a referendum on our continued membership of the EU.

The TV news and Spanish papers covered the UK election, which surprised me, we don't hear much about elections in Spain, or any other European country. Our media are focused on the US, if they can be bothered to look abroad. One national daily referred to us as '*la isla excentrica*' - the eccentric island. Not too bad, there are worse things to be called. They are concerned that a British exit would weaken the EU that has done a lot to accelerate the development of Spain since the death of Franco.

*

The next day was dull, all on road to Mansilla de las Mulas. At least the weather was better than expected and we had little rain. No mountains were visible in any direction, not even little hills. The major landscape features were modern and man-made - big bridges where railways and roads crossed each other. The fields were green with crops, mostly cereals, stretching to the horizon, broken up by scattered trees and woods. Pia complained it looked just like Brandenburg.

So what's a scientifically minded mathematics graduate doing on a medieval pilgrimage route? The medieval mind seems alien to me, credulously believing in dubious miracles and even more dubious relics. I'm with Newton - 'O Physics, save me from Metaphysics'. To me, the purpose of scientific enquiry is to clear away superstition from both organised religion and new-age spirituality, and reveal what, if anything, remains. Mystery does remain, of course. We can deduce the Atapuerca cave man lived a million years ago, but did he have a human soul? If not, when did that come in? Science is not an excuse for rejecting the spiritual - the revelations of science are, very surprisingly, even more fantastic and awe-inspiring than the imaginings of poets and priests. Newton himself had spiritual beliefs, ones he had to keep to himself as they would have been considered heretical at the time.

Perhaps it's the attraction of opposites - the medieval and the scientific. Reaching 60 brings an increased awareness of mortality, which is one step closer to the medieval. The camino provides time for meditation, immediate awareness of the here and now, awe of nature, contact with people outside one's usual circle. The medieval is emotional, and communal.

Our fellow travellers included devout Catholics, lapsed Catholics, the 'spiritual but not religious', the curious, people seeking quiet time off the treadmill to find a new direction in life, people who just like nature, history and a nice long walk, and even lapsed vegetarians and a couple of not very strict Muslims. I never encountered any kind of intolerance, anything other than acceptance. *The company of those seeking the truth is infinitely to be preferred to the company of those who think they've found it* (Terry Pratchett, *Monstrous Regiment*)

*

In Mansilla de las Mulas both the albergues seemed crowded so we took a private room. Even Saint Brierley (shock) suggested the possibility of taking the bus into Leon the following day. However, for the sake of completeness we walked, and with better weather and expectations lowered it didn't seem too bad. Around Arcahueja we were away from the road, but instead of continuing over a green hill that would have made a fine approach to the city the way turned left and took a more urban route. There were pedestrian bridges over the *autopistas* and N-roads. As we walked through an area of apartment blocks, feeling out of place, people surprised us by cheering and wishing us 'Buen Camino' as we passed though their neighbourhood, as if we were doing something mildly heroic like running a marathon, raising our spirits.

We came at last to the old city. Why are these old cities so appealing? Am I allergic to the 20th, or even the 21st, century? Not really, it's just that they are so pedestrian-friendly compared with modern cities, a joy to walk through. Old buildings of local stone built by hand on a human scale, as opposed to intimidating towers of poured concrete. Without any discussion, we have given over our streets, that used to be communal places, completely to cars. It's changed just in my lifetime. When I was young children would play football in the street. That was normal. Nowadays, the people that live on the street would tell them off for damaging their cars, and the police would tell the parents off for allowing their children to play in a dangerous place.

We checked in for two nights into a double room at the Hotel Boccalino in a good location on the Plaza San Isidro. We do like our rest days. We were on the top floor, and from our balcony could just see the towers of the cathedral. Round the corner was a building designed by Gaudi, across the square was the San Isidro church and the 'Pantheon'. There seemed to be a lot more to see here than in Burgos.

In the hotel common room we bumped into a friend of John's, the tall Australian I had last seen downing strong drink at the bar in Calzadilla. She told us that he had had serious medical problems, and had been to hospital in the meantime, pissing blood. John appeared, in good spirits as ever. She had bought him a simple mobile phone in case he had any emergencies. I don't know if he made it to Santiago, this was the last time we ever saw him.

Outside the cathedral we bumped into the Polish man we had met at Fromista. He was still only able to walk with a stick, but had obviously recovered enough to leave the albergue and travel by train to Leon for his last days before returning home. He was now accompanied by a Polish girl, who also spoke English. The cathedral itself appealed more than the one in Burgos, not having been divided into so many chapels and retaining the feeling of being one harmonious whole, with brilliant stained glass windows. It nearly fell down in the 19th century. It must have been a major technical challenge to repair and replace the interdependent cracking arches and walls on one side without the whole lot collapsing like a house of cards, possibly requiring more careful thought before doing anything to it than building the whole thing from scratch originally.

Sitting in the back of the San Isidro church during mass we met Kate and Kelsey, whom we hadn't seen since Fromista. They had taken a few rest days because of blisters and then taken the bus to catch up with their schedule again.

The existing church is 'only' about a thousand years old. The original church was built in a time before the Muslim invasion of Spain, on the site of a Roman temple to the god Mercury. I was struck by the Pantheon next door, where the Kings and Queens of old Leon (nothing to do with the rock band) are buried. The colours on the ceiling, described as a Romanesque Sistine Chapel, are, for some reason, just as brilliant as when they were first painted. They reminded me of the ceilings of Byzantine cave-churches I'd seen in Cappadocia in what is now Turkey, from the same era. Stylised depictions of saints, without perspective, and inscriptions in Greek as well as Latin.

*

Walking out of cities never seems as hard as walking in. It's just as many miles, but it's cool in the mornings, and the streets are very quiet. The Spanish are not up and about as early as the pilgrims. We paused outside the ornate renaissance Parador San Marcos, taking photos alongside the life-size statue of a medieval pilgrim. We came across many such statues on the camino, all very life-like, inviting modern pilgrims to stand alongside them. We pressed on through the city streets, navigating the brief green alternative branching off at Piva Motor and returning into the suburb of La Virgen del Camino.

The route branched again immediately. We took the green (and older) route via Mazarife, heading for an overnight stay in a vegetarian albergue, only the second one of the trip so far. For some reason, they are much more common in the later stages. I started to get excited about the scenery again - I could see mountains with snow on to the north, the Picos de Europa.

We arrived at the albergue on a warm afternoon. Those who had already arrived were lying around in hammocks and on sun-beds, looking very relaxed. We checked in, set up our beds in a big dorm, and had our showers. We decided it was time to machine wash all our clothes (actually we had done this once already in Logroño) and get them properly clean. It only cost a few euros to use the machine here, drying them on the line. I met Guillaume, from Lorient in France. He had walked several caminos over the past ten years. He explained to me, in a mixture of English and French that he didn't work, indicating something wrong with his head, I'm not sure exactly what. He said the first part of his life had been very bad, but now life was good.

Chores done, we went to rest in the garden. We'd been lying there a short while when Guillaume leaped off his lounger, announcing loudly to us he'd had a good sleep and was going off to look round the village. People around him looked annoyed. It hadn't occurred to him other people might be trying to catch up on their sleep too. I don't think he realised how loud he was, or noticed how annoyed other people were. I thought he looked like someone with Aspergers, although it could have been some more serious mental problem now under control with medication, I'm not an expert. I think he liked to talk to me because I didn't seem to get annoyed, at least not as quickly as others. I'd seen it before, including possibly in myself as a young man.

The veggie meal didn't start well for me - a bowl of raw green things, with no dressing. Even the tomatoes were green, but it got better later. When Rachel had finished her bowl of green things, I swapped it for mine, which I'd mostly just played with.

This was the first time I encountered Walther, from Switzerland. I was impressed with the way he could effortlessly switch between speaking German to the man on his left, amusing the two Italian ladies opposite him in their language, and carrying on a conversation in English with ourselves and the two Finnish women next to us. I asked him what he did for a living and he replied that he was a gastronome. That was a job title I hadn't come across before. Instead of trying to construct a joke about Swiss gastro-nomes that he'd probably heard before anyway, I asked him what a gastronome did. Was he a chef, did it involve tasting lots of good food? He said he managed 30 chefs. Just as well our hosts didn't know that.

Also in our dorm were a bunch of lively young American students from an English language university in Rome, several Germans of a certain age and naturally a higher than usual proportion of vegetarians.

*

The next morning, we approached a village, Villavante, where according to the master Brierley there was a bell-ringing competition every year in August. Sure enough, as we entered the village there was a board with information in Spanish about this festival. We ring bells in our local church. Bell-ringing in England, like most things, is done differently from the way it's done on the continent. The bells are mounted on wooden wheels with ropes on the outer edge of the wheel rigged to allow 'full-circle' rotation, and thus enough control, if you have the skill, which is harder than I thought it would be to acquire, to time the motion precisely enough to make the traditional peals and changes with their distinctive melodies. As opposed to just going Ding-Dong.

We walked into the main square and stopped, looking up at the clearly visible bell-tower. I could see three bells, mounted on wheels but with what looked like chunky bicycle chains instead of ropes, presumably allowing them to be moved back and forth by an electric motor. They would have to disconnect that mechanism, maybe even change the wheels, to allow manual ringing.

An old man in a black beret shuffled across the square towards me. He must have seen the cogs going round in my mind. He started speaking, slowly in Spanish. First he invited us to guess his age. I thought about 80, but guessed a bit lower to be safe. He laughed. He was 92. 'Soy el mejor campanero', he said - 'I am the best bell-ringer'. That was the only complete sentence I understood. That didn't bother him, he carried on talking. I only got fragments. I got the idea that in the good old days the bells were always rung by hand, by men, but nowadays it was done by a machine, or, even worse, by women. I tried to tell him we were bell-ringers too.

You can't plan moments like that, and they don't happen at all if you move too fast without time to linger and let things happen.

We entered Puente de Orbigo over the strikingly beautiful bridge that gives the village its name. It's also remarkably long for a medieval bridge, must have been an enormous project 800 years ago. And it's still carrying traffic today. Which of our construction projects today will still be useful in 800 years time? Actually, it's an enlargement of a Roman bridge built by the engineers of the Seventh Legion 2000 years ago. All hail the engineers of the Seventh Legion. *Sinistra, dextra, sinistra, dextra...*

We walked through the town, passing a number of albergues, heading for Verde, another vegetarian albergue. You wait ages for a vegetarian albergue, then two come along at once.

Again it was a warm afternoon and people were

relaxing in the large garden. Well, not everybody. Lots of young people were working hard in the field attached to the albergue. They have land, and grow their own organic vegetables. I didn't envy the people working in the warmth of the afternoon. I almost felt guilty, lying there watching them. People ask if you become exhausted on the camino, walking day after day. Not at all, never felt better. It's an easy life, you don't have to cook and you don't have to clean, just walk and take care of yourself.

The albergue was full and the dorm was crowded, but with interesting people. I was glad we'd arrived early enough to get in. The *hospitalero* asked me why I drank cow's milk, inviting me to try rice and other kinds of vegetable milk. I suppose the answer is simply received culture, especially in my case as my father was a dairy farmer. He was quite passionate about what he believed in, in this case veganism and animal rights. This was the only time on the camino I was ever 'evangelised', that anyone tried actively to change my opinion on anything. I don't mind, he was clearly sincere. I certainly never encountered any intolerance or bigotry of any kind on the camino.

Before dinner we were offered the chance to do yoga with a teacher. I had never been to a yoga class in my life. I decided to try it, aware of the fact I should be careful with my legs. I needed them, every day. I realised I would not be 'good' at it - I'd never done it before and I'm not naturally flexible -

but that's not the point. The teacher, a Spanish man of my age and hippy appearance, who had studied yoga in India, put us at ease, quickly spotting my lack of experience and offering me an extra cushion. The emphasis was on 'mindfulness', awareness of the body, breathing and the 'here and now', and relaxation, rather than stretching and attaining positions, though there was some of that. We were asked to remove our watches. I lost track of time, and was shocked at the end to discover two hours had passed. In the final session of meditation, our teacher played guitar and sang, I think in Sanskrit, at least I heard the word '*Rama*', meaning God, repeated. Finally, he told us the Sanskrit word for peace is *shanti*, and to remember we were walking the *Camino Shanti-ago*. I thanked him afterwards, and told him that was my first ever yoga lesson, at age 60. He was happy about this, and urged me to continue yoga when I returned home.

We were privileged to be there on an evening when they were cooking something special. People were in the tiny kitchen all day making a 'vegetable sushi' - vegetables in rice wrapped in spinach leaves. There was a hearty soup before this. A thoroughly enjoyable veggie meal at a crowded but lively table. We first met Ulrike from Germany here. A French mother and son sat opposite me, a Canadian to my left and another unrelated French father and son to my right.

*

After a crowded breakfast we set off across countryside far from main roads towards Astorga. After a few hours of remote countryside we came to a wayside stall where a Spanish man called David offered food and drink in return for *donativos*, donations. He lived up here in this remote place in a sort of shack with a stove. His washing was drying on a line between trees. His only link to the outside world was a scooter. Spiritual advice was painted on the stall '*La llave de la esencia es la presencia*'. He must watch the sunrise and sunset alone in this remote place, a very different experience from the crowded albergues of the camino.

After resting and drinking in the shade, we pressed on to Astorga, a walled town on a broad, low hill, founded by the Romans. There was much to see there, but we were tired at that time of day and opted for lunch in the Plaza Mayor, busy with regular tourists and locals as well as pilgrims. We noticed pictures in shop windows of Denise Thiem, the pilgrim who had gone missing, last seen in Astorga four weeks before. Despite the temptations of the chocolate museum we went on.

Just before Murias de Rechivaldo, where we were heading to, a woman with a clipboard stepped out from an orchard onto the track ahead of us. She indicated she was deaf, and showed us the clipboard. There was a list of names and addresses, all different countries, supposedly people who had each given ten or twenty euros to the deaf charity she was collecting for. The amounts seemed large, I couldn't imagine lots of people giving twenty euros to a complete stranger in the middle of nowhere without even any kind of identity, badge or uniform. I smelled a rat. I learned later, from the camino forum, that this was indeed a scam. Quite a good cover, pretending to not be able to speak, if you have an accent that might identify you, give you away. It's probably unrelated, but it struck me as sinister that the only place on the whole camino where I encountered anything that could be seen as criminal activity was on the section where Denise Thiem disappeared.

We stayed the night at the albergue Las Aguedas, at the far end of the village of Murias de Rechivaldo. Here we met Terry from Belfast, who was to be our companion off and on from here to Santiago. He was on his second camino, and had written a book about his experiences on the first. The camino was harder for him than for us - he wasn't a regular walker at home, despite living in Ireland, which has loads of mountains and coast for walking. He found the hills and mountains something of an ordeal. But he was far more of a true pilgrim than we were.

He told us of an albergue at the next halt, Rabanal, where he'd stayed last time and was dying to stay again, warning us not to take the last place before he got there. This was Refugio Gaucelmo, run by the Confraternity of Saint James from London, so English speaking. It was popular with people from many countries curious to try the afternoon tea and biscuits served in the garden.

*

The next day we climbed on minor roads and dirt-tracks above the 1000m contour. We were approaching the Montes de Leon that form the western rim of the meseta. We entered El Ganso and beheld, and had a drink in, the Cowboy Bar that we recognised from the French film 'Saint Jacques - la Mecque' about three siblings on the camino. We saw this film even before we saw 'The Way'. I'd already enjoyed two other films by the same director - Coline Serreau. This film concerns two brothers and a sister, not very nice people either to each other or to anyone else. They are brought together after years of estrangement by the death of their mother. It is a condition of their inheritance, set by their mother, that they must walk the camino together. Each night they must stay together in the same albergue. Their *credencials* would provide proof or otherwise of this. For any of them to inherit, all of them must complete the walk, so they must help each other. None of them are walkers, and they seem to hate each other.

Reluctantly, they undertake the pilgrimage. As they progress along the way, they change and become better people. I thought, I could do with some of that. At the end of the film, as they walk away together from their mothers' house, having presented their *credencials* to the lawyer, the ghost of their mother is seen looking down on them from an upstairs window, blessing them.

We didn't get half of it, the French was too fast and there were no subtitles, but we got the idea.

We arrived early in Rabanal. It was a short day even for us, only 15 km. When we arrived Gaucelmo was still closed, so we looked round the village and sat in the Santa Maria church. We came out shortly before the albergue was due to open and saw there was already a crowd gathered outside. It was operating at reduced capacity, only 20 beds, and we were lucky to get in. Terry was in the queue, otherwise we would have been in trouble for taking the last place. A German woman that we knew, Gisela, was initially turned away on the grounds that she had sent her pack ahead. Some of the albergues have a policy of being only for 'true pilgrims', that is, not for 'tourists' who have their bags transported, only accepting those who arrive on foot with their packs. She didn't seem to understand what he was saying, in English, possibly deliberately. Unfortunately for her the warden not only spoke Spanish (despite being English) but German as well. Eventually he relented on the grounds that she was over 70, so it was reasonable she was having her bags transported.

Afternoon tea in the garden - the first of the three really good cups of tea I had in Spain. There was a community of German Benedictine monks in the building next door (that's the sort of thing you find yourself saying on the camino), some of whom joined us for tea, young men. They invited us all to join them at Vespers later in the church we had sat in earlier.

The service was in Spanish, German and English. The little church was full, mostly with pilgrims. Rachel and I joined Terry near the front. As a result, I got invited to deliver the reading in English. I moved to sit with the monks, and one lady, conducting the service. They sang psalms and prayers in Gregorian chant. I'd been given the order of service, as it contained the reading, and I prepared by considering it, deciding how to phrase it, what to emphasise. The order of service also contained the music for the Gregorian chanting done by the monks. I could follow that too, I'd done workshops on Gregorian chanting at folk festivals I'd been to. At the end of the service the priest asked us, when we returned, to weave at least 15 minutes a day of meditation into our daily lives. He reminded me much of the yoga teacher at albergue Verde.

After the service Terry congratulated me on my reading. He said I was a better Catholic than he was. Not true. Not true at all. Afterwards the three of us went for a meal with Glenn, a Canadian man who had lived most of his life in Thailand.

*

The next day we went 'over the top' of the Montes de Leon to Acebo. Not many places to stop, only two in fact, all day, but we were now above the agriculture amongst pine forests and wide expanses of purple heather. We met a man coming the other way, back from Santiago, with a donkey and a dog. The dog was riding on the donkey, enjoying the adventure, the man walking behind. We climbed up steeply through woods until we came to Foncebadon, a village that looked like it had been completely abandoned, fallen down a bit and then come back to life with the revival of the camino. Half a dozen of the old farm buildings had been converted into albergues, the rest continued to fall down. We stopped for a coffee and an orange-juice, then carried on. Our luck with the weather was holding in the place where it was most important - the top of the mountain.

We came to La Cruz de Ferro, the very highest point on the whole of the camino, an iron cross standing over a huge pile of stones. You're supposed to carry a stone with you on the camino that means something to you, and leave it there. It could represent troubles you want to leave behind. Of all the stories I've heard about these stones, Terry's was the best. I say the best, it was far from being a happy story, but it was the most appropriate. He was carrying a stone from the ruins of a church in Belfast that had been burnt down by an angry sectarian mob.

The contemplative atmosphere around the stones was punctured by the arrival of a big party of Brazilian cyclists, eager to be photographed en masse by the stones, punching the air in triumph. I suppose to a cyclist getting to the top of the highest mountain on the route is something to celebrate. But there was a completely different spirit about them, the size of the group, the triumphal attitude. I'm not saying it's wrong, I'm just saying it's a different culture from that of the solitary pilgrim on foot. Not all cyclists are like that, for example the two also from Brazil who were at Acacio y Orietta, but many seem to be in a different world even though they stay in the same albergues.

I was carrying something, but not a stone. I was carrying a Saint Christopher made by my aunt from pewter a long time ago. She had carried it on her journeys, and when she got too old to travel she gave it to me, as I seemed to have become a bit of a traveller, like her. I've carried it for about 25 years now myself. I know she once went to Lourdes, even though she was Anglican, and would have wanted to do this herself in her youth. Rachel thought I should keep it, so it could keep on protecting me. This didn't feel like the right place, perhaps too pagan for her. I didn't encounter anywhere suitable in the cathedral in Santiago either, and I decided Rachel was right.

At Manjarin we stopped for coffee and Terry again caught up with us at the simple albergue run by Tomas, a modern Knight Templar and the one and only resident of this almost abandoned mountain village. The path dropped steeply and roughly down to Acebo, just a normal mountain path to us but to those only accustomed to city streets, like our friend Terry, a daunting prospect.

We stayed in the modern albergue at the far end of Acebo, built with a view over Ponferrada. It was a combined pilgrim albergue and tourist hotel. For only 10 euros each we got a bed for the night, a balcony with a view of Ponferrada and the mountains and use of big but chilly swimming-pool. Not what I expected on the camino. Rachel went for a swim but not me - I can cope with heat but I get profoundly cold very easily in places like that.

The western edge of the meseta is actually bordered by a double range of mountains - the Montes de Leon that we had just crossed and a second range that lay ahead of us, the western end of the Cordillera Cantabrica. We could see the whole lie of the land from here, the Cordillera Cantabrica about two days walk away, the intervening plain and the city of Ponferrada below us. There was a Templar castle in there somewhere, but from this distance the city was dominated by a single ugly black skyscraper, shaped like a game of Jenga. I wonder who the architects were on that one.

Our little dorm had only 8 beds, and there were only two other people in our dorm, both from California. On the balcony I got talking to a young man from the next dorm who was a truck driver from Hungary who spoke English with a Yorkshire accent, probably because he now lives in Keighley. The Californians belonged to a hiking club that were rattling along the camino at a much faster pace than us, about 35 km every day. It was too fast for Gen as well (one of the two in our dorm). I suggested she walk with us the next day to Ponferrada and then catch a bus or taxi on to catch up with her friends. She seemed very pleased with that suggestion. She didn't feel comfortable about walking alone.

Gen was originally from Laos, of Chinese ancestry, and went to America when a teenager as a refugee from the Vietnam war. When she arrived in America she couldn't even read the Roman alphabet, but now she had a career in writing software, like I used to. I suppose in software the cultural differences would matter less. As we walked the next day she told us much more about her life, things she said she doesn't normally tell people, despite the fact we were strangers.

There was one aspect of our life-style at home that intrigued Gen, like many Americans. Although we own a car we rarely use it, perhaps once every couple of weeks. Even then it's for social purposes - going to a dance, or going hiking. The shops are at hand, there are a few buses and trains to the big cities and the internet for most other things. We can even do pleasant walks right out of our front door.

*

The walk down from Acebo was very attractive as far as Molinaseca, natural paths, forests and wild places, rustic villages. We had our usual coffee and orange-juices in Molinaseca. The last 7 or 8 km into Ponferrada was hot and even the 'green' route was almost all on road. It turned out to be the hottest day of our camino. To Gen it wasn't hot, she was from Los Angeles and anyway she liked it hot. We walked with her to the tourist information. When we were all satisfied she could get a bus to where she was going we said our good-byes. We never saw her again. Such is the camino.

We found a room in a hotel, allegedly the last one. From our room on the top floor we looked directly across the Plaza Encina to an intact 12th century castle of the Knights Templar, the *Castillo de los Templarios*. We looked round the castle in the baking heat of the afternoon, a taste of what it must be like in summer. There was an exhibition of illustrated medieval books and, of even greater interest to me, maps. It was getting hard to walk round outside, the air was filled with white stuff like cotton wool blowing in the breeze. which may have been tree pollen from lime or linden trees. It found its way inside buildings wherever doors or windows were open because of the heat.

*

We were able to get breakfast ridiculously early and were on the road by about 7am, a record for us. Even cities are pleasant to walk through at that hour. Just as well, the first 10km were mostly along roads, admittedly very quiet at this hour. But our destination was a world away, a rural idyll, and a vegetarian albergue to boot. Happy wife equals happy life, as someone once said to me. Probably my wife.

We arrived at El Cerbal y La Luna (The Rowan and the Moon) at the start of the heat of the day, and spent most of the afternoon in a sort of swing chair in the shade. It occurred to me this rural green landscape was much like Wales, only much hotter. It turned out the young *hospitalero*, Gareth, was from Betws-y-Coed. He didn't sound Welsh, probably because he'd been living in Spain with a French girlfriend for three years now.

All the other pilgrims there were women. We met two women who had been there a few days with problems with their legs. It's surprising, you would think that if you had walked 600 km already with no problems, as we all had, that you would make it the less than 200 km to the end, but no, pride, or feeling smug, comes before a fall. This happened to a surprising number of people. With no warning they got pains in their feet or legs that stopped them completely. The name *plantar fasciitis* is often banded around in the albergues.

Possibly people sensibly start at a moderate pace, then after they feel they've got used to it, and that they've made the transition from an office job to walking a long way with a pack every day, they increase the kilometres. And then something goes wrong.

The two women were Paige from London and Rita from Finland. There were also two Polish women that we saw at a few albergues along the way, and quite a few Germans. Rita helped Gareth with the cooking, and we had a wonderful meal together. After the meal, we started drifting back to the dorm, cleaning our teeth etc.

I had imagined that on the camino there might be evenings where people took it in turns to do something, sing a song, tell a joke, whatever, to entertain each other. I hadn't heard that it was a camino thing, but have encountered it on other long trips. Sometimes a bottle is spun and whoever it points to has to get up and do something. It helps if you have drunk the contents of the bottle first. I'd even prepared a few songs just in case, something slightly appropriate like a couple of verses of 'Spanish Ladies'. But it didn't happen, not even in Galicia. There were albergues where there were guitars lying around, like here, so maybe sometimes.

Two cyclists came in, both male. One spoke to Gareth in Spanish. I thought it was odd, but I could understand everything he was saying. Eventually, Gareth and the cyclist realised they were both Brits, and why didn't they speak English, much to everyone's amusement. The cyclist needed somewhere for his dog. Yes, these two men were cycling the camino with their dog. We went to bed.

We were woken in the night, or at least Rachel was, by the sound of a dog crying, very close by. In fact, it was just the other side of the wall from where our bunks happened to be. Very unfortunate, Rachel is not exactly a dog-lover at the best of times. It would have to be next to her. Gareth is a very accommodating young man who doesn't like to turn anyone away, but the dog was a bit of a problem. It couldn't be left outside because the village dogs run loose at night, and they don't welcome strangers, and dogs are not allowed inside the albergues, so Gareth put it into the barn next to the dorm.

Rachel went to wake poor Gareth, who had already been kept up late drinking with the cyclists. Gareth woke the dog-owner, and persuaded him to sleep in the barn with his dog. This seemed to make the dog, and therefore Rachel, happy, and everyone slept happily ever after.

*

We got up in the morning and went for breakfast at the time we thought we had been told, 7am. No sign of Gareth or any breakfast. We gave him some slack and went back to pack our bags. After another half-hour, still no sign. Eventually, someone woke him. He had, understandably, overslept, and produced breakfast as quickly as he could. When we left, later than planned, later than most albergues even allow you to stay the cyclists were still sleeping.

It didn't matter as the next day was cool with grey skies, just like home. We found the green route to Villafranca del Bierzo. Some of the vineyards were covered in what looked from a distance like snow, but was actually the white stuff that had been blowing around in the heat two days ago. We left Villafranca on the Alto de Pradela route, that used to be the main route. No-one followed us, everyone else slogged up the N-road to Trabadela. Our route was more strenuous, an extra climb of 300 to 400m, but it was exhilarating, with views up the deep green valley to the mountains around O Cebreiro. I can see why you would take the road if you were behind time or had physical problems, but otherwise, if you have the time and you're fit, there's no contest.

At the end of the Alto de Pradela we dropped down steeply into Trabadelo, rejoining the main route. We had a coffee with a Chinese lady, and then set off up the road. The road-walking confirmed my feelings about taking the high route. Admittedly it was quiet, there was hardly any traffic, which was good. The new A-6 had taken almost all the traffic. Some of the time this new *autopista* towered over us on stilts high above the valley, sometimes it was close by, at our level. As we approached La Portela de Valcarce we came to a place that I thought couldn't be right. We were walking without any protection on a slip road for the *autopista*, unable to see far because of the bend in the road. I've checked this out since, and it was right, that is, it is the official route. Even Google Earth Street-view shows pilgrims at this spot. It was only dangerous for about 50m, but even so.

There was a choice of vegetarian albergues further up the valley, but that would have made the day too long. We decided to stop at the albergue El Peregrino - The Pilgrim. It looked like a roadside motel from the outside. The lady that ran this place, which was also the village bar and, indeed, a motel, was very good to us, letting us have a room with two bunk beds and an en-suite bathroom for no more than normal albergue rates. Other pilgrims, including some couples, were already in small dormitories. I thought we were just lucky to get this room, but Rachel thought she gave it to us because she was amused by my attempts to speak Spanish. There may be some truth in this, as at the evening 'pilgrim' meal she did seem to be on a mission to teach the pilgrims, from many different countries, to speak some Spanish.

*

The next morning, as we left La Portela de Valcarce we left the N-road, and according to the Codex Brierleianus we wouldn't be near one again for four days of walking. Good news. The *autopista* was soon out of sight as well.

It does say something about the camino that this is a cause for celebration. Most long-distance walking routes necessarily cross national roads, but they try very hard not to follow them. The camino sticks to them like glue in places. In more remote areas we could see miles of countryside with a network of broad farm tracks either side of the trail, or miles of forest and mountains to left and right, but the camino was on, or close to, a country road. Every country has different rights of access to countryside, and I don't know about Spain. My guess is access rights are non-existent in the countryside outside of national parks. The country landowners would have been on the winning side in the Civil War. Spain does have beautiful national parks of course. The Picos de Europa spring to mind, but the camino does not pass through any of these. The camino is, of course, not just a long-distance walking route, it's something special.

We had the best, and also the biggest, breakfast of the whole camino at El Paraiso del Bierzo, at the entrance to the village of Las Herrerias. We'd walked further than usual before breakfast in the cool of the morning, so we'd worked up the appetite to do justice to it. A large group of American students came in, saw us enjoying our hearty breakfast, and ordered the same. We declined the offer of horses to take us to O Cebreiro, and began the big climb up on an old mule track until we reached - Galicia.

GALICIA

A huge stone tablet announced the entrance to Galicia, the final region on our journey. I had thought of Galicia as a Celtic region, the name being related to 'Gaul' and 'Gaelic', but the language is a variant of Spanish, actually closer to Portuguese. The definite article, which had mutated from 'el' to 'lo' in Leon, now dropped the 'l' sound completely to become simply 'o'. This gave place names and signs a misleadingly Irish sound, like the first village we came to, O Cebreiro.

O Cebreiro was an attraction for a few mostly Spanish tourists as well as being on the pilgrim route. There were reconstructions of traditional round dry-stone walled houses with thatched rooves and a large old dry-stone walled church. When I say old, I mean the building was from the 9th century, the oldest church on the camino. It had been sheltering pilgrims from the cold mountain winds for well over a thousand years. The sound of bagpipe music came from a few tourist shops, enhancing the 'Celtic' atmosphere. This was just CDs playing. In fact, the lack of real traditional music in Galicia was to be something of a disappointment for me. I had imagined something like the west of Ireland. We had the first of many *caldo gallegos* (hot cabbage and potato soup, which may or may not be vegetarian) in the café of a small hotel. The equivalent of the *municipal* albergues in Galicia were those run by the x*unta* (association, pronounced 'shunta'), and there was a 104-bed *xunta* albergue in the village. It was only lunch time and it was too cold to sit around, so we decided to press on instead to the next village, Alto do Poio. We were fortunate to have great views in all directions as we walked along the top of the purple heather-covered mountain. It's frequently shrouded in cloud, and raining heavily. As late as mid-April the paths had been blocked by snow.

There was only one place to stay in the tiny village, and it was filling up fast. The dormitory was crowded, only sixteen bunk beds but quite close together, and only two shower/toilets between us, so when the queue of pilgrims arrived in the afternoon we were all over each other trying to make our beds, unpack, shower, wash our socks, get to the toilets etc. When we'd all done what we had to do I could see 14 of the 16 beds were taken. We retired to the bar to pass time till the time for the evening meal but, as was often the case in the mountain villages, the bar was very cold with the wind blowing straight through it. The only warm seat, by the stove, was firmly occupied by the proprietor's mother. So we went back to the dorm for a while to warm up.

A man walked into the dorm. I'd already noticed him a few days earlier in the trail. He had a habit of passing the Albergue where we had decided to stop that day, or maybe stopping with a friend for a cold beer before going on further into the warm afternoon, but we'd see him again, a day to two later. I noticed him because he had a strikingly different style from most other pilgrims, at least from the neck up. Instead of the usual sensible broad-brimmed hat against the sun he wore what looked like a check tea-towel worn Arab style around his head. Combined with dark sunglasses, a swarthy complexion and several days of stubble he reminded me of the SAS soldiers behind enemy lines in Iraq in the BBC film version of Bravo Two Zero, except that he didn't have an enormous pack and was only lightly built.

When he walked in, I actually sympathised with him. He went to one of the two remaining empty bunks, the top bunk on my right. The older, Spanish woman on the bottom bunk was not pleased at this, and immediately warned him not to *molestar* her things. She'd spread all her things all over the floor on both sides of the bunk. I couldn't see how he could even take his pack off and sit down without touching any of her things, never mind unpack and make his bed, and he'd just walked in tired and hungry from the mountain. She had probably been hoping to have the bunks to herself, and was slightly disappointed to find a hairy, sweaty man was going to be sleeping on top of her.

We went for our evening meal in the bar, leaving him to sort himself out, and get to know the lady in the bottom bunk.

When we returned, a few hours later, most of the others were going through the usual rituals, cleaning their teeth, getting their gear ready for the morning and settling into bed. The little anteroom before the dormitory, no doubt an overspill area on busy summer nights, was now occupied by a large dog, much to Rachel's disapproval, that was walking the camino with her mistress, an Italian pilgrim from our dormitory. Outside, the three Alsatians belonging to the proprietor circled the building. Beyond them, the village dogs roamed the night. Large dogs turned out to be a feature of rural Galicia.

When the time came for lights out, there was only one person missing. He must have carried on drinking with his companions from the bar. The bar had closed at lights out, but his companions had private rooms. We turned out the lights and hoped for the best. It was to be a memorable night.

I was woken some time around midnight not by our friend, who I could just about see was still missing, but by a commotion at the other end of the dorm. Someone, I never did see exactly what they looked like, was coughing violently and loudly, unable to stop or control themselves. When I say loud, I mean I was wearing earplugs against routine snoring but was blasted awake by the outburst. He was struggling to catch his breath, but managing to shout and swear in desperate sounding German, occasionally bellowing 'I'm sorry' in English. People around him were trying to calm him down, making helpful suggestions involving 'wasser' or 'agua'. At first I felt annoyed (I like my sleep) but then realised that wasn't a very noble feeling. The man plainly couldn't help it and was in some distress. The disturbance continued for what seemed a very long time but I'm told was about 45 minutes. Even when things quietened down I couldn't get straight to sleep, fully expecting it to start again.

I went back to sleep. About an hour later I was awoken again, but more subtly. To my left, someone was snoring in French, but otherwise it was silent. I had become aware that Rachel, in the bunk above me, had become agitated, and the light from her little torch was flickering around the room. I opened my eyes and could make out the figure of a man standing and waving his arms about. It was the missing pilgrim. At first I thought he must be sleep-walking, or mentally ill. I watched him for a while. He was silent, but reaching out with his arms and very unsteady on his feet. He was drunk. He must have had very poor night vision, I could see him by the dull glow of the emergency lights but he clearly could not see what was in front of him. He was feeling his way around, trying to find his bed but having forgotten where it was.

He found the door of one of the toilets, went inside and didn't reappear for a while. I had almost dozed off again when he reappeared, this time minus his trousers. He continued the search for his bed. Unable to find his own, he tried some other people's. By this time everyone was awake.

Eventually he found the one bed that was empty, but this was not actually his bed, where his sleeping bag was. He climbed the ladder to the top bunk, lay down, fell asleep, and immediately started snoring.

I dozed off again. I was awoken by a crash. He had got cold in the night, remembered he had a sleeping bag somewhere else and decided to go in search of it. He had not remembered he was on a top bunk. The Brazilian man in the bottom bunk was dimly awoken by an unexpected scrabbling around in the bunk above him, which should have been empty, and opened his eyes only to see a body tumbling past him to the floor. Being light, young and drunk, after a moment the body arose, unharmed but very bewildered.

Rachel kindly intervened at this point, shining her little torch on his real bunk, with its welcoming sleeping bag. The drunk looked delighted, climbed the ladder, holding on tight this time, and surprisingly managed to find the right end of his sleeping bag. He got into it, promptly fell asleep and immediately started snoring again.

When the time came to leave in the morning, everyone else in the dorm, except him, had already left. We were often the last ones out. It was only about 8am, but that was the time you were supposed to leave by, to give the *hospitaleros* time to clean, ready for the next batch of pilgrims who would start to arrive about lunch time. He was still sound asleep, dead to the world. He wasn't actually dead - I could still hear him snoring.

They say you see the real person when someone is drunk. If that's true, he wasn't at all a bad person. He was never loud, or aggressive. Only confused. Very, very confused. We expected he would pass us sometime, but we never did see him again.

*

The next day we left the mountains behind for the last time. At breakfast in the albergue in the next village we caught up with the party of young American college students we had met at breakfast the day before in Herrerias, before O Cebreiro. We descended to Triacastela where the Australians Dave and Sue were searching for an ATM to relieve their cash flow problem. From here we had a choice of routes and, unusually for us, we opted for the main route, on the grounds that it was both more direct and greener, that is, there was more walking away from roads. The alternative had more accommodation and a historic monastery at Samos. We now had a choice of two vegetarian albergues to aim for. The one at A Balsa was way too soon, so we pressed on to Paloma y Leña.

We were lower, and the day was hot. At one point, anxious to find the turning off the road which was described as difficult to spot, we turned too soon and went up an unnecessary hill. We retraced our steps. As the day wore on I'd almost run out of water when I saw what looked like a mirage - a vending machine in a field, dispensing chilled drinks, miles from any road or human habitation. A single power cable ran off into the bushes. I put in a Euro and - it worked, a bottle of ice-cold water.

Even so, time was passing, and there wasn't much accommodation on this route. In fact there wasn't any apart from Paloma y Leña unless we walked on to Sarria, at least another 8km at the end of a hot day. I got out my mobile to phone ahead to the albergue and braced myself for another attempt at a telephone conversation in Spanish. This time the *hospitalero* spoke perfect English. We managed to reserve the last two places. Phew.

Paloma y Leña seemed like a paradise, especially compared to the previous night. We arrived all hot and tired. Everybody else, we really were the last two to get in, was relaxing in hammocks, reading, having a cold beer or a hot tea. Children were playing, and chickens were wandering around. Even the cats were too laid back to hassle the chickens. We met a Dutchman who had walked from Saint Jean but been afflicted with crippling pains in his feet and ground to a halt seemingly within striking distance (just over 100km to go) of Santiago. We also met Norbert from Germany, the self-styled 'camino pessimist'. I felt for other people who arrived after us and were turned away, having to walk a hot 8 km in the afternoon sun to Sarria. The dormitories were full, but not crowded, with plenty of showers and toilets. There were computers I could use. I could even pay by debit card.

The highlight was the communal meal in a grand dining room, a hearty three course vegetarian meal with red wine, as much as you could eat or drink, and good conversation around the table. There was a spirit about the place - calm, communal, tolerant, you could say spiritual even though that wasn't explicit in any way, and yet efficiently run.

*

We expected a change in the character of the walk the next day, which would take us through Sarria. Sarria is the last place you can start and still qualify for the Compostela. You have to walk at least 100 km to Santiago. So many, particularly Spanish, pilgrims start from there. I'd read the paths would be much busier.

We didn't notice any change. If anything the paths seemed quieter, even though logically there must have been more people walking the stages. The reason is, the stages are much more well defined from Sarria onwards. Almost all the beds are in a few relatively large towns spaced about one days walk apart. But we walked out of step with this design. We passed through Sarria, the starting point for these masses, about lunch time, and continued, with some difficulty, to find beds out of the few that were available at the in between places.

The language in Galicia is noticeably different, closer to Portuguese in fact, but guessable if you know the Spanish word. In places we would see old road signs that had been 'corrected' by an enthusiast with a spray can of paint, for example from *iglesia* (church) to *igrexa*. The 'x' was pronounced 'sh', so that xunta (council, or association) would be pronounced *shunta*, the equivalent of *junta* in Castilian, that is standard, Spanish. Modern road signs were in Galician.

By now there were stones marking the route and displaying the remaining distance to Santiago every kilometre. We felt a childish excitement at the numbers counting down below 100, at what seemed like an ever-increasing rate. Excitement, and also sadness that the way of life into which we had settled so comfortably was coming to an end.

We passed a young man in a wheelchair, propelling himself, accompanied by a young couple and a dog, all bound for Santiago.

Some said you needed to get 2 stamps a day on your *credencial* to get a *compostela.* All the way along, we had only got the stamps from our overnight accommodation. Enthusiasts would collect extra stamps in churches and bars along the way. We chose not to, the *credencial* was inside the pack where it was safe from rain and wear and tear, and anyway it would fill up too soon if we did that, putting us to the trouble of getting an extra one. They were only obtainable in the big cities. This extra requirement didn't seem to make sense to us, so we ignored it. The *compostela* is after all only a piece of paper. We will always know what we have done.

At Ferreiros, between Sarria and Portomarin, we stayed in a shiny modern albergue in deep countryside. We recognised 4 of the 10 people we were sharing our dorm with - two Finnish ladies and an elderly Swedish couple. There were also two youngish Spanish men, an Austrian couple (the man was the largest person I saw on the camino, and as I feared, a heavy snorer) and two other men, a German called Klaus and a Frenchman called Pierre. Klaus was quite large too, and Pierre warned me his friend, who was in the bunk next to ours, snored. Rachel quipped she could reach across and poke him if she had to. Pierre paused for a moment, and said 'No, if you do that he will only start snoring again. You will have to kill him'. Pierre had a dark sense of humour I hadn't encountered before on the camino, except possibly in Norbert the 'camino pessimist'. Pierre and Klaus had walked together all the way from Saint Jean, and the previous year from Geneva to Saint Jean. We got to know them better in the village bar later on. Both were very successful businessmen. Klaus had a factory in China and an Indian wife. Pierre was married too, with international business interests. I was intrigued how they had managed to be so successful and yet take so much time off. They said by employing and delegating to the right people. How they managed to take so much time away from their wives I didn't enquire, in case Rachel took it the wrong way. They were both planning to meet up with their wives in

Santiago at the end.

*

The next morning, we made an early 7am start, and skirted the town of Portomarin. We heard that every bed in Portomarin had been taken the previous night, so our strategy of avoiding the main centres was working, but it was worrying that as the season advanced (it was by now mid-May) the albergues were becoming full. What could it be like in summer? Again we found a bed in a small country place and this time a good night's sleep. A simple pleasure, but the previous three nights had been punctuated either by loud snoring or the shenanigans at Alto do Poio. We dined at a small table of friends old and new, including Ulrike from Germany and Christine from the USA.

The next night in the town of Melide we opted to stay in a private double room in a pension, partly because we'd spent a string of nights in dorms and partly because all the good albergues in Melide were full by the time we got there. The country towns in this part of Spain were not so beautiful. The ancient cores of the towns were tiny, often only an admittedly remarkably ancient church, the surrounding town appearing to have been built, fairly cheaply, since the 1960s, obliterating whatever else was there before. The pension was all we hoped for and the landlady friendly and personal. She also worked behind the bar in the associated bar/café where we had our breakfast early the next morning. Staying in these towns and venturing out in search of (vegetarian) food in the evening gave us an experience of the 'real Galicia', off the camino and a challenge for our limited Spanish.

The countryside surrounding these towns was indeed beautiful rolling green gentle hills, never flat but no dramatic views, the glimpses back to the purple mountains we'd come from coming less and less often. It was well wooded, with eucalyptus starting to appear amongst the pines. The farm and village houses were built of local stone and what looked like slate rooves, unlike the red tiled rooves elsewhere. A green and pleasant land. The Shire. In fact, pilgrims with their back-packs and beards even looked like hobbits from a distance. The farming was noticeably different from the rest of Spain, dairy farms that looked and smelled like the farms in mid-Wales or western England. Even the dogs were different from the rest of the walk - every farm and most houses in the countryside had one or more large dogs, always tied up if they were by the camino, but watch out if you wander off anywhere else.

*

There wasn't much accommodation a day's walk beyond Melide. We started early, and when we stopped for lunch at a café we tried to phone to book in at the albergue at Salceda, but could get no reply. We got talking to the café owner, and she recommended a place called 'The Way' that I had ruled out because it seemed too far away on my map. It turned out to be 2 km closer than was indicated. I phoned to book for Rachel and me, and also for Ulrike who was having lunch with us. While I was on the phone two pilgrims we'd never met before turned up, similarly concerned about finding accommodation and asked me to increase the booking to 5 people, to include them. This phone conversation was easier than expected, because as the name of the albergue suggests, the owner was English. This all turned out to be very fortuitous. We walked past the albergue at Salceda on the way, and it seemed an unappealing place on the main road. 'The Way' at Brea was much more pleasant, and offered us the second of the three really good cups of tea we had in Spain.

*

The day had now arrived for our final approach to Santiago. We considered staying the night in the huge 400-bed hyper-albergue on the slopes of Monte do Gozo, entering the city itself the next morning. With hindsight, that might have been a better idea, but we thought it seemed a dull and soulless place to stay when the enchanted city itself beckoned. We set off, mostly pleasant eucalyptus forest to start with but with more and more hot asphalt as the day wore on, past the airport and on. The approaches to the big cities always seemed to take longer and be more tiring than expected, probably because I wasn't really paying attention to the distances marked on the map and thinking 'let's just get there'.

We were delighted to bump into Paige again, the woman who had seemingly broken down with leg problems over a week earlier in El Cerbal y La Luna. She was obviously going strong now, walking faster than we were, and was going to make it. She told us of a German couple she had seen on the camino 'having a domestic', as she put it, with 'sticks flailing'. This would have stood out on the camino, most people you meet are quite calm and laid back. After this we often saw a couple and wondered is it them? Are they German? Have they had a row or do they naturally walk that far apart?

Saint Brierley warns we all experience different emotions at the end, not necessarily what you're supposed to feel. This turned out to be prophetic. As we arrived at Monte do Gozo, the 'mountain of joy', it seemed a far from joyful place. This is supposed to be the place from which the medieval pilgrims first caught sight of the city and the cathedral, and wept for joy. Brierley, optimistic and upbeat as ever, omits to mention this view is now obscured, possibly by the cupressus trees behind the tacky kiosk. A huge monument of rust and concrete commemorates a visit by Pope John Paul. We stopped and rested with a cold fizzy canned drink from the tacky kiosk, and were delighted to see our old friend Christine from California arrive. She was alarmed we had not booked accommodation in Santiago. I wasn't worried because it was a week-day, it wasn't high season and anyway my wife wanted to walk round and look at a few places before we committed to three nights in this special place.

Some concern flickered in my mind. We decided to move on, after visiting the old chapel, the only place that could be described as 'spiritual' or evoking a sense of history. The camino signs pointed straight on. I hoped we might come to a viewpoint, or somewhere more atmospheric. Instead, the way plunged straight down the hill, past the big albergue and into the nest of busy dual-carriageways circling what appeared to be an entirely modern city. With hindsight, which is a wonderful thing, I should have ignored the camino sign that clearly indicated 'Santiago' and instead followed the sign saying 'Albergue'. We walked through this noisy hot nest of roads for about a mile until we came to the edge of the suburbs. A pilgrim asked me to take a photo of him. I though he meant where we were standing, but we crossed a busy road so I could take a photo of him in front of the 'Santiago' road sign. The sign itself was dirty and covered in graffiti. After I'd taken his photo, he offered to take mine, and seemed surprised when I declined. I didn't want a photo of this place.

I crossed the busy road back to rejoin Rachel. We headed on, negotiating some big city roundabouts. By the time we passed through the Porta do Camino into the old city, we were hot and tired. I was disappointed we still hadn't seen the cathedral. I had imagined the towers beckoning us onwards, and us getting more and more excited as we drew near. We stopped and rested in a café, but this didn't seem to improve our mood much. We carried on. The towers appeared above us, and soon after the cathedral itself. It was all a bit much, the crowds of happy pilgrims and tourists, the heat, an awareness that I was definitely not feeling what I was supposed to be feeling and the concern that we needed to find somewhere to stay.

I suppose we were too concerned with sorting out the practical details. The same 'protestant work ethic' that drives us to work and save for the trip, to learn foreign languages and even write this book makes us too bothered about being efficient, too anxious about the mundane, too busy, and stopped us feeling what perhaps we should have been feeling.

The search did not go well. We started with the somewhat arrogant idea we would walk round to find a hotel that looked nice in a good location in the old city. We were quickly disillusioned. Hotel after hotel was *completo*. Sometimes the staff offered dodgy and overpriced propositions that added to our feeling that this was a serious problem. We gave up the search and headed, still wearing our back-packs in the late afternoon heat, to the tourist information in the Rua Vilar. We waited in the queue to see the young man at the desk, another thirty minutes passing before we reached the front of the queue. A sign on the desk warned he was only a trainee.

He was wonderful. He asked exactly what we wanted. Rachel said ideally a private room with a bath, for three nights, but we were desperate for anything at this stage. He told us straight away what we'd just spent 2 hours finding out laboriously, that the old city was full. He made a quick phone call and found exactly what we wanted, only 5 minutes walk outside the old city, a combined hotel and albergue called La Salle. This was to be our home for the next three nights.

We'd paid the price for not carrying a tablet or smart-phone. We could probably have squeezed into an albergue somewhere, but, as in the other major cities en route, we had chosen to go a bit upmarket for our rest day, at least as far as a cheap hotel or pension. It's easier to do the research on a tablet in a quiet half-hour in an albergue than it is to walk around a city with a back-pack. It's easier to check availability and make the booking on-line than to make numerous phone calls, quite possibly in another language. And on top of that, though it seems unfair, you may well get a better rate through an intermediary like booking.com than if you phone directly or simply walk in off the street.

We'd landed on our feet in Burgos and Leon, earlier in the year. In Pamplona we had booked on-line in advance, before we set off, and got a better rate as a result. Only in Santiago did we come a bit unstuck, although not for long.

*

The hotel was next to a convent and quiet except for the bells. That's alright, we like bells. We walked into the old city, clean and refreshed after a good night's sleep, in the cool clear air of morning. There was definitely more magic in the air today. We went to the Pilgrim Office and queued for our *compostela.* I presented my *credencial* to the young man behind the desk and filled in the form. The form asked age, nationality, occupation, where we started, all the information needed not only for the *compostela,* but also for the statistics published by the Pilgrim Office, which I find interesting. These figures show the phenomenal increases in the numbers of pilgrims in recent years, and the distribution throughout the year, with more retired people in spring and autumn and a huge number of students and young people in the summer. Most interestingly, they show the numbers from what seems like every country in the world. Spain is top of the list naturally, with Italy, Germany, Portugal and the United States following, Ireland, the UK and Korea not far behind.

The *empleado* didn't spend much time perusing my *credencial.* Instead, he looked me up and down and decided I just looked like someone who had walked 800km from Saint Jean. I was lean, bearded, booted and suntanned. He filled out the *compostela* and handed it over, congratulating me.

I thanked him and we went to the cathedral,

happily bumping into our friend Christine again. She offered to take photos of us clutching our *compostelas* in front of the east door. It was morning so that was where the sun was shining, and anyway the west door, the place most people finish and normally more photogenic, was having restoration work done on it. We spent quite a bit of time inside the cathedral, soaking up the atmosphere and history in the early morning quiet. I did indeed hug the big statue of Saint James himself. Well, it made me feel better. Eventually we went out into the old city and explored the back streets, including the daily search for veggie food.

We bumped into Pierre, the Frenchman with the dark sense of humour that we'd met in Ferreiros, a few days before. He was now with his wife, who had flown in to be with him in Santiago. I asked him what had happened to Klaus, his snoring camino companion. 'I had to kill him', he said.

In the afternoon we returned to La Salle to use the hotel computers. We had happily not made any arrangements for our return to England. It was time to do so now, and plan the rest of the trip. We felt it was more, what is the word, appropriate?, spiritual?, poetic? to return home overland. It might be cheaper and faster to take a budget flight, but there's nothing less poetic than a Ryan Air flight to Stansted. If you live in the north of England, it's not even that practical landing at Stansted at Ryan o'clock somewhere you can't get out of to anywhere except further south to London.

We were fitter and healthier than we started, and more surprisingly the trip was costing less than expected. We had quite a few days left on our 60-day insurance policy, and decided to use all of them. We planned to do the walk to Finisterre and Muxia, with a couple of rest days somewhere on the coast, catching the bus back to Santiago. Then the early morning train via Palencia to Santander on the north coast and a spare day in Santander. From Santander there is a regular ferry across the Bay of Biscay all the way to Plymouth in south-west England. I booked the ferry first, making sure of the international connection. Then the advance train tickets, incredibly cheap. It's all so easy on the internet.

That was enough, no need to plan the details of the walk to the coast. I'd left plenty of time for it. I didn't try to book the train tickets onwards from Plymouth. I'd already worked out before leaving England there were no advance cheap tickets on this leg (and they were over three times as expensive as the Spanish trains for the distance) and anyway we couldn't be certain when the ship would get in.

That evening, we returned to the cathedral for the evening mass where we knew they would be lighting and swinging the *botafumeiro*. This is the mother of all incense burners, swung high over the heads of the worshippers and tourists, having been hoisted aloft and set swinging by 8 strapping *tiraboleiros* in red robes. The service was in

Spanish, and we are not actually Catholic, but it held our attention. A nun taught the congregation to sing an anthem consisting of alleluia and simple Spanish, simple enough for me to join in heartily with that bit.

Afterwards we went for a meal with Ulrike, another German called Peter who was flying back to Germany the next day, and Dave and Sue from Australia. We had 'pilgrim meals' together, the last time for Peter, in a restaurant in the old city. It was an old, characterful place, with dark wooden paneled walls all around. When we'd finished eating and taking each other's photos, a man burst into the room dressed as a medieval monk, singing out loud in Latin or some kind of old Spanish, I'm not sure which. Having got everyone's attention, he proceeded to tell stories and make a kind of fiery drink. When I say fiery, I mean it was actually on fire in a huge bowl in front of him. He was adding spices and strong spirits, ladling it up and letting the flaming liquid pour back down into the bowl, while continuing to sing and shout and tell what felt like very scary stories. A woman came into the restaurant with group of friends through a door just behind the monk. Turning her head from talking to her friends she suddenly caught sight of a mad monk singing and playing with fire, and screamed. Everyone laughed, her friends and those already in the restaurant. Shock turned to embarrassment as she realised this was just part of the show. Not quite the cool entrance she had hoped to make, but credit to the acting and charisma of the 'monk'. The drink was called Queimada, and is a speciality of Galicia. We were invited to have some of what the 'monk' had just made. It was gorgeous. Reminded me of 'rum and raisin' ice cream. I had loads.

Santiago is supposed to be where you reflect on the journey to this place, a magical place to some. At times around the table, when I wasn't actively taking part in the conversation, I found I was reflecting on a journey, the journey of my life from a difficult and unpromising beginning to being accepted in this company of seasoned travellers and intellectuals of many nations, being able to pass for normal, or better still, interesting. But that's another story, another book.

*

The next morning, our last in Santiago for a while, we returned to the cathedral for some more 'quiet time'. When we came out we by chance bumped straight into Terry! We hadn't seen him since Cruz de Ferro on top of the Montes de Leon 11 days before. He was struggling then, and we hadn't seen him that night in Acebo. I had been looking out for him wondering if he was alright, and whether he would make it. He had literally just finished his camino there at the west door of the cathedral. He was in tears, partly I knew because it was the anniversary of the death of one of his sons. A true pilgrim, far more than we ever were. He was so much the true pilgrim that a crowd of tourists gathered to photograph him. He didn't seem to care.

He was feeling all kinds of emotions, including a longing to get back to his wife in Belfast.

That evening we bumped into Paul, one of the five young Germans we had often encountered in the early part of the walk. They got ahead of us later, and Paul was spending his last night in Santiago having already walked to Finisterre and come back on the bus, the situation we would be in, in a week's time.

There was no doubt we would walk on beyond Santiago if we could. In Britain, it being an island, long-distance walks inevitably end at the sea. If you haven't got to the sea yet, you haven't finished.

*

We walked out of Santiago early the next morning, passing the north face of the cathedral and the magnificent Hostal dos Reis Catolicos built as an albergue in 1492 but now an upmarket hotel. In less than a mile we were in woods, with a beautiful view behind us of the sun rising above the towers of the cathedral, that we looked at for some time. That's more like it. Such a contrast to our entrance to Santiago.

We walked on quiet country roads and forest tracks through an undulating landscape of villages, farms and forests, similar to what we had experienced since we left mountains for the last time at Triacastela, just before Sarria. As we travelled further and further west, towards the sea, eucalyptus appeared more and more in the pine forests. At Negreira we stayed in a modern but almost empty albergue on the edge (San José) but had our pilgrim meal and passed the evening at another much busier albergue in the centre of town.

*

Next day we walked to Maroñas and stayed at the café/albergue Santa Mariña. We'd met Walther again that day in a busy café at lunch-time and seen him phone ahead to book there. There were only 10 places according to the guide-book, so I decided to do the same. Walther was surprised to see me attempting Spanish on the phone. Walther was in a 6-bed dorm with a group of 4 Spanish people. We were allocated a 4-bed dorm to ourselves. Lucky again. One of the Spaniards spoke good English, and introduced himself and his friends saying, with a smile, 'We are opera singers, but we only sing at night. I am the bass. My wife is the alto'. Rachel wasn't sure what to make of this, but I knew what he was hinting at. I said we had plenty of ear-plugs. He said that was good, we would need them. It was Walther that had to suffer the snoring, we had a cushy night.

The Spaniard offered to make us a cup of tea. We thought he was just trying to humour us because we were English, but said yes out of politeness. The tea was excellent, the last of the three really good cups of tea we had in Spain. He was a tea enthusiast, and was not fooled by what passes for 'English tea' on the continent - Liptons. He had lived, worked, and learned his English in Leicester as a young man.

At our evening meal Walther revealed to us why he was walking the camino. He was wrestling with the decision whether or not to become a Benedictine monk, like the ones next to Gaucelmo at Rabanal. I would never have guessed. An urbane, multi-lingual gastronome. He would make his final decision on his return to Santiago. We'll never know what he decided, we lost touch after this evening. I would say he probably did.

We had to decide, less critically, about the next day's walk. A fork in the path lay ahead. Not as much as it did for Walther. We could either go to Finisterre first, or Muxia (Moo-shee-ah). Because of a gap in the albergues, going to Finisterre would mean a 30km day followed by a short one. Going to Muxia first would allow us to maintain our steady 20km/day rhythm that had been so successful so far, so we opted for the Muxia route, hence parting from our friend Walther, who perhaps needed to be on his own.

*

We started off the next morning, the weather fine but cool. We'd been so lucky with the weather. Galicia has a reputation for rain, it's where the Spanish go to escape all that heat and enjoy bucket loads of rain in the summer, but we hadn't had any for weeks. Santiago gets on average more rain than Manchester. And Manchester has more miles of canals than Venice, and so on.

Monte Aro stood above us, not exactly a mountain but certainly the highest hill around. The camino followed the country road on the north side. We took Brierley's green alternative which would climb almost to the top and would be a break from the road-walking. Soon after we turned we were harangued by two barking dogs that ran through their gate out onto the road. Their owner came out to tell us, in Spanish, we were going the wrong way, indicating back to the camino we had intentionally left. I said we were going to 'Monte Aro', pointing to the hill. I didn't understand what she said, but she didn't seem convinced. I was confident because I'd seen a wooden finger-post with Monte Aro written on it pointing our way, and the dogs were troubling Rachel, so I broke off the conversation and carried on.

The walk panned out as Brierley described it, ascending to wind turbines and gaining long views. Still no sight of the sea yet. On the way down we did miss one right turn. Actually we saw it but didn't quite believe it, as it was neither marked nor taken by anyone else wearing boots recently. We carried on down, realising from the map a couple of right turns would get us to the same place. We ran into another pair of dogs loose on the road. This time I was not able to persuade Rachel to go past them, so I had to do some seat of the pants navigation on roads not on Brierley's map to get back on track.

We never had a problem with dogs on the camino itself. Even Rachel wasn't afraid of what she called 'camino dogs'. They saw so many pilgrims every day they couldn't be bothered to bark. But go off the camino, especially in Galicia, and it's different story, even on public roads.

After lunch in Olveiroa there was very pleasant walking on a high open hill through heather and pine. It came as a shock that the fork in the path was so unpleasant. I knew it would be high on the open moors and expected it to be somehow more picturesque. When I got there it was a big modern roundabout with wide fast roads in all three directions, and nowhere safe to walk, no *senda*, no hard shoulder, no 'natural earth path', nothing. The moor itself was rough, made even rougher by the recent construction or 'improving' of the roads. This continued for a mile after the junction until we got onto safer and more pleasant off-road paths that took us down to Dumbria, for our last night before the coast.

The very modern combined albergue and village hall was open when we arrived. Curiously, we only saw the *hospitalero* for about half an hour while he checked people in. The rest of the day and night we and the other pilgrims were trusted to take care of the place ourselves. This included getting our breakfasts (things we bought in the village shop when we arrived) and letting ourselves out in the morning.

We had the biggest *menu peregrino* of the camino in the only place in town, the restaurant/bar of the hotel O Arxentino. It cost a couple of euros more than usual, but it was worth it, it had quantity and quality. It was the only time I couldn't eat everything that was put in front of me. Just as an indication of the quantities Rachel's veggie second course (having already had a big mountain of tuna salad) consisted of four fried eggs and big plate of chips.

I should mention the puddings, always a topic dear to my heart, that we had in Galicia. Either side of Santiago these we usually *'tartas de Santiago'*. This was a cake, heavy with almond essence with an outline of the cross of Saint James dusted onto the top with icing sugar. Basically a Bakewell tart (is there an ancient connection I wonder) without the jam, which doesn't sound that exciting but it was always so freshly-baked and tasty. I never got tired of them.

*

The next day, we set off through forests, excited by the prospect of reaching the sea. We met quite a lot of people coming the other way. Most go to Finisterre first. Many finish there, but others carry on along the coast to Muxia and then come back the way we were going. Some walk all the way back to Santigao. I had the extra challenge of following Brierley's directions in reverse.

We reached the sea in the early afternoon, at a white sand beach under a hot sun, with a cold wind blowing from the north. Muxia was visible a couple of miles away across the bay, but it would be much further on foot, and there were still a couple of hills to climb.

When we arrived in Muxia we met Ulrike, waiting for her bus back to Santiago, to catch her plane home to Germany. She was to be the last of our camino friends that we saw. They'd all gone home now, and anyway we were sort of dropping out of the camino now, staying in private rooms, more like a couple on holiday. But we would still share meals with new people, and meet them on the way.

Muxia oddly reminded me of Llandudno and the Great Orme, on a smaller scale. The sea was on two sides of the town, east and west. And it was cold and windy. We did the obvious walk to the end of the prominent headland to the north, a pilgrimage site in its own right. There are stones here, one shaped like a sail, the whole said to resemble a magical boat. It was where Danny's ashes were finally scattered by his father in the film 'The Way'. It was blowing so hard we didn't dare go to the stones themselves to crawl under the 'sail'. We found a spot out of the cold wind and in the sun, where we could linger and take in the sea.

We stayed only one night, deciding to spend our rest days all at Finisterre. It was worth going to Muxia, to the very end of the peninsula, but it was too small a place to stay any longer. We also decided to make things easy for ourselves by splitting the 30km walk to Finisterre in two by stopping at Lires.

*

We left Muxia, rather ambitiously following Brierley's notes in reverse. We dropped down to the beach at Praia Lourido, despite a Spanish man telling us that was wrong, we should go along the road. So far we were following Brierley backwards, but we exited from the beach too far along and came to the village of Lourido, where the village dogs had turned out to greet us. Passing this, with difficulty, we saw signs pointing up a steep track to Monte Lourido, heading south, and took that route. It was a strenuous but exhilarating climb to the top, the day was cold with grey skies, so we didn't get sweaty going uphill, and the view from the top was possibly the best I had on the camino. I could see no certain safe way down on the north side, so we backtracked the way we had come. Actually, if we had been bolder we would have found perfectly good tracks on the north side that rejoined the camino. This cost us a lot of time, but was fun, apart from passing those bloody dogs yet again. We had plenty of time to reach Lires, I wouldn't have taken such 'adventurous' decisions if we hadn't.

The rest of the day was on country roads and forest tracks, not exactly on the coast but with views of sea and hills. We could see headlands that at home would be criss-crossed by footpaths, but not here. There's much less population, and possibly less tradition of pedestrian access to beauty spots. We crossed the Rio Castro on the new bridge, passing the now defunct and admittedly dangerous looking stepping stones, and came into Lires. Paul, the young German we last saw in Santiago had given us a tip about a house on the beach, but the phone number we had didn't seem to work. No worries, we stayed at the excellent Casa Luz, dining and passing time at the new albergue nearby, watching the sunset over sea at the extraordinary time of half past ten. We were starting to stay up a bit later now.

Spain is of course in the west European time zone that is one hour ahead of the UK, the same as France and Germany. We were now so far west it would actually make more sense by the sun to be one hour behind. Add in the effects of summer 'daylight saving time', and the result is that man-made time is nearly three hours out of sync with natural time by the sun. Sunrise, even now, was about 7am. The sun reached its highest point in the sky not at midday but at about 3pm, and the very hottest time of day, when your washing should be on the line, was from about 4pm to 7pm.

*

Next morning, we had our breakfast, said goodbye to Yolanda our hostess, and set off on our very last full day of walking. So sad.

We took the green slightly longer route along the estuary, passing the house on the beach we had been told about. Someone else had stayed there that night, we saw them packing up as we went by. We approached Finisterre, or Fisterra as it is spelt locally in Galicia, clearly a headland on a much larger scale than Muxia.

The day was hot as we walked the final part of the walk along the road, Fisterra ahead of us, the beach of Praia do Langosteira to our left, and the sea beyond. It seems incredible, but when we got back home we read that a 20 year old German pilgrim had died in that sea, swimming from that beach, that very same day, presumably as we were walking only a mile or two away, with no idea what was happening. He was alone and the alarm was not raised until the next morning when his clothes were found on the beach. Shocking turn of fate, to have come so far, to be so nearly there, so nearly safely home again, and then be understandably tempted to go in the sea to celebrate or cool down.

Completely unaware of this unfolding tragedy, we carried on, preoccupied with the tricky business of finding the *hotel rustico* we had booked for our last three nights. We took a room with a picture window view across the bay to the west and settled in.

The walk down into the town of Fisterra was steeper than any section of the camino, and I slipped a couple of times even in my hiking boots. On the way down, we went past an Alsatian chained up outside a house. I looked at it (Rachel is nervous of dogs) and saw it was on a very short chain. It looked back at me silently, with sad eyes. I had the feeling this was not a happy dog, that no-one ever threw a stick for it or took it on a long walk.

We found a hippy café very much to Rachel's taste, with lots of veggie and Indian food (La Frontera), at least for the day-time, for some reason they didn't do evening meals. From the café we could see the pilgrims arriving or leaving on the Santiago bus, the central albergue and the harbour.

On the way back up to the hotel we passed the house where the dog should have been. We could see it loose in the street about a hundred yards further ahead of us. It was dragging the short chain behind it, dangling from its collar. It's a funny thing but when we go on walks at home dogs are often attracted to me. I've even known them leave their owners and follow me. It came bounding up to me. I felt it could smell the rest of Spain on me, and wanted me to take it for a really long walk. It jumped up, and although I felt it wanted to play they say you should never put your hand out to a strange dog, so I didn't encourage it.

It then jumped up at Rachel, putting its jaws around her arm, in play. I told Rachel to stay calm and, much to my surprise, she did. The owner shuffled out of her house in her dressing gown and called the dog, which ignored her. She tried to grab the chain, but the dog moved just out of her reach, showing neither love nor respect. We moved on up the street, leaving her ineffectually chasing after the unhappy dog.

*

The next day we set off for Cabo Fisterra, the end-of-the-world itself. Our hotel was well placed to walk directly up to the high level path along the spine of the peninsula, avoiding the road that most people take from the town to the cape. This path is an old Roman road for much of the way, and they weren't the first to be drawn here. There is evidence of habitation a thousand years before them. The Celts made offerings to the sun at the stone 'Altar Soli' up on Monte Facho, the hill we were crossing. In the distance we saw the light-house and made for it. We took photos by the stone 'KM 0' marker, and continued, past the light-house to the 'fire-pit'. Apparently, the thing to do is to take off your clothes, burn them, go into the sea naked and come out a new person. Not sure what you're supposed to do then. Very poetic, but not very practical. We were still high up on the headland, far from any beach. This was as far as we could go without falling off a cliff. Naturally, we stayed here a while before heading back to the town.

Et tout là-bas au bout du continent,
Messire Jacques nous attend,
Depuis toujours son sourire fixe,
Le soleil qui meurt au Finistère.
(words from 'Ultreia' by J. Claude Bénazet)

In the town some Irish pilgrims asked me where was the end of the Camino Finisterre. It never occurred to me to think about it before, it was obvious to me the way ended at the cape, when you could go no further. But I knew the official end was the central albergue in the town, and was able to direct them. It's hard to spot the albergue, unless there's a queue of pilgrims out of the door, never mind realise that spot is the official end of a camino. It surprised me people need to be told where the end is - the end is wherever you want it to be.

Wainwright, a name not known outside of Britain but a local hero in the north of England, once wrote a book called 'A Coast to Coast Walk' describing an excellent walk from the Irish Sea, through the Lake District and across Yorkshire to the North Sea, of about 200 miles. I've done it myself twice, once each way. In the Preface he explains he has deliberately called it 'A Coast to Coast Walk', not 'The Coast to Coast Walk', encouraging everybody to work out their own way using the Ordnance Survey maps, taking in places that matter to them. I've met people more than once, clutching his book, who have told me in all seriousness I wasn't doing it properly because of some variation I'd put in. I simply take the book off them and point to his words in the Preface. Saint Wainwright was a predecessor of Saint Brierley.

Surprisingly, medieval pilgrims also continued beyond Santiago to Finisterre, picking up their own scallop shell from one of the beaches to take home and wear forever as a sign of what they had done. It is even believed that in pre-Christian times people would make the pilgrimage to this westernmost point of the known world to make an offering to the setting sun.

I can believe Saint James died in Palestine in 44 AD, but the transfer of his body to Santiago seems more legendary and miraculous than historical. The shrine was not 'discovered' until the early 9th century, the start of the medieval pilgrimage. However, there was a man from Galicia called Priscillian, a devout 4th century Christian 'Doctor' (Latin for teacher, the same as Guru in Sanskrit). Priscillian's practices and theology did not quite square with those of the increasingly assertive Roman church at that time. His practices included vegetarianism, although not for the same reasons as most modern vegetarians. He was eventually tried and executed for heresy and sorcery at Trier in France. But in Galicia and northern Spain he was still seen as a martyr, not a heretic. His body was indeed brought back from Trier to Galicia, and the number of his followers increased dramatically. Priscillianism was only stamped out in the 6th century. Priscillian has the distinction of being the first man in history to be put to death in the name of Christianity. Actually, it's impressive that the early Christian church ran for so long, over 350 years, before going so clearly off the rails. Political parties struggle to make it to the next election without contradicting their principles. To be fair, the Pope at the time, Siricius, was not happy about this, the trial and execution were by secular authorities. The cult of Saint James may have been founded to overwrite this earlier episode of church history.

*

The time came to pack up and head for home. The bus to Santiago was shiny and new, almost full of returning pilgrims, three hours (the driver said it was two) without, of course, a toilet. One final evening, for old time's sake, in the ancient streets around the cathedral at Santiago. An early morning departure from La Salle, walking at first through the old city, under the statue of Cervantes for the last time, down streets that had become familiar, then more mundane streets out to the train station.

The train journey was magnificent, the scenery even more spectacular than on the the walk, mountains, lakes, forests. The line went through remote areas of the mountains, rejoining the camino at Ponferrada with the distinctive ugly black skyscraper. From then on it was a recap, on and off, of the camino. More mountains, then as we approached Astorga, a view of the extensive city walls. As the train slowly pulled away from the station we passed under the camino bridge, where pilgrims zig-zagged back and forth up one side of the railway line and down the other. To us arriving in Astorga the bridge had just seemed amusing, but now the weather was hot and we could see many more tired looking pilgrims making their way over the bridge, as we had done three weeks before. After Astorga the city of Leon, all the time the train gliding along comfortably between stations at over 160 km/hour. After Sahagun the train again left the camino heading south to Palencia, where we got off and changed trains. Another train took us north again, crossing the camino at Fromista, where we went right past the converted railway building where we had slept in a room next to Kate and Kelsey over a month ago now, and onwards descending through even more mountains, down and down from the meseta, to the coast at Santander.

*

We had 24 hours in Santander, a safety margin to ensure catching the boat home. We saw and chatted to the occasional pilgrim doing the Camino del Norte. Santander wasn't at all dominated by a camino in the way the cities of our camino were. There were no brass scallops set into the pavement. People stared at the handfuls of oddly dressed pilgrims on the streets. I had noticeably more difficulty communicating in cafés, waiters spoke fast and were not at all used to foreigners of any kind. We wandered around the centre of town, looking inside the cathedral, going for a ride up the *teleferico* (funicular railway), watching the families playing in the park and looking across the sea to the headland on the other side. The Guardia Civil put on a show, well a training exercise really, involving men abseiling from a helicopter into a boat and transferring between speedboats and rubber dinghies. Workers were swarming all over a new silvery building being constructed on the waterfront.

Our huge ferry lumbered into the harbour and tied up. I couldn't help noticing that after 50 years of feminism, possibly fewer in Spain, all the construction workers on the glistening new edifice were men, and the long line of cleaners waiting to go on board the ferry before us were, as far as I could see, all women. The cars and caravans streaming off were almost all British registrations, most of them heading further south than we had been. A smartly dressed officer in uniform greeted us as we stepped onboard with '*Bonjour*!'. I was momentarily confused, we were in Spain, bound for England, I'd been struggling with Spanish for weeks, especially here in Santander, and now an official looking person was addressing me in French. Of course, it had slipped my mind, the ship was French - the Pont Aven, belonging to Britanny Ferries.

We settled into our little cabin, put on our warm clothes then went up on deck to watch the ship pulling away from the shore, and the sunset. The ship pulled further and further away from the darkening coast of Spain, the lights of the villages becoming clearer as the night fell.

*

The next morning, after breakfast, we went up on deck again in the bright sunshine and cold wind. The coast of Brittany itself approached. Actually, we entered a narrow passage between the island of Ouessant (Ushant in the song Spanish Ladies, the song I never did get to sing) and black jagged rocks and islets. This surprised me, I thought we would go round to the west of Ouessant, well clear of the rocks. The ship must have about three decks below water-level. Putting our faith in GPS, the map-makers, the engines and the ship's computers we ploughed through.

The next land we sighted was either side of the entrance to Plymouth harbour. The four warships anchored in a line to starboard reminded me of my last visit to Plymouth over 30 years ago, as a civilian contractor working inside the Navy dockyards. We didn't know at this point whether we would get home the same night or not - it was late in the day and although I knew it was just possible if we got ashore quickly I should not be anxious about it, or disappointed if we had to stay the night here and carry on the next morning. We got off the ship and through immigration (there wasn't any queue for 'immigration' on top of the Pyrenees) fairly efficiently, and took a taxi the one mile to the station, only to increase our chances of catching the last train that would get us home that night. The taxi got stuck in the rush-hour traffic, and was possibly no quicker than walking would have been. We bought our tickets, many times more expensive than they would have been in Spain for the same distance, and caught our train.

The scenery along the coast of Devon from Plymouth to Exeter was as beautiful as anything in Spain, the sun sinking low over the sea. Two men from Liverpool got on, going back to their families for the weekend after working the week in Exeter. We were travelling up through Somerset, and I was saying to them about our trip and how well all our travel arrangements had gone when, in an uncanny echo of our journey on the TGV from Paris to Bayonne nearly two months before, there was a scraping sound from under the train, and we ground to a halt in the middle of the countryside.

The driver announced that some 'person' (to put it politely) had thrown a bicycle onto the line in front of the train. Eventually men arrived to inspect the underside of the train. We went on a bit, there was a burning smell, and we stopped again. It was decided to move us all into the front few coaches and carry on to Birmingham. The bike had sliced through cables affecting brakes and other things on the rear coaches. By the time all this had been decided (this involved mobile phone calls to bosses on a Sunday evening, not the best time to get hold of them) a couple of hours had elapsed. It looked like we were not going to get home that night.

One advantage of this happening at such an off-peak time was that there were plenty of seats in the front coaches deemed to be OK. Off we went. At Birmingham we were put on a train to Chester, as we had planned, and told that because we would get there too late for the last train to our final destination the train company would pay for taxis. And refund, in vouchers, our expensive train tickets. I actually felt sorry for the train company, it wasn't their fault some idiot for no reason threw a bike in front of one of their trains, seriously damaging it.

Our final destination was the station we had walked to at the beginning of this story two months ago, about 4 miles from our home. I'd hoped that if at Chester we were put in a taxi to our final station, we could then persuade the driver to actually take us all the way home instead. But our final station was on the way to Liverpool, and we were put in the same taxi as the two 'Scousers'. We couldn't divert it without delaying them, and they were tired and wanting to get back to their families.

We were dropped off by taxi at the deserted country station at 1am. We could have tried to get another taxi, but we had our walking boots on our feet, all our gear was neatly stowed in our rucksacks on our backs, just like on the camino. The moon was full, and shining brightly down from a clear sky. It was dry and still, the ground looked like it had not rained for some time. This was the way our camino was meant to end. We started walking.

We reached home about 2:30am, not at all tired. The moonlit garden looked wildly excited to see us. We performed our rituals for the containment of bedbugs, not that we had any, involving large plastic bags positioned ready for us in the porch, and entered the house.

I kept my camino beard for a week, until everyone had seen it, and then shaved it off for the summer. Friends asked if we were 'recovering', imagining that it must be difficult to walk 500 miles or more. No, actually we're deteriorating, now we're back to a more sedate life-style. I never felt better than on the camino. We never had a single blister, or any other walking ailment. We're both quite healthy for our age, but what few minor troubles we may have had seemed to get better on the camino. As if it was rejuvenating.

People commented how well we looked, and how happy. We were lean and suntanned. Our friends seemed very pale compared with our fellow pilgrims still fresh in our memories. The once familiar streets of the town where I was born seemed different.

And the end of all our exploring
Will be to arrive where we started
And know the place for the first time.
(T.S. Eliot)

Transformation? Not exactly, not this time, more

a correction, away from materialism, away from worrying about things that don't matter. But things will never be quite the same again. Certainly not my perception of what is 'walking distance'.

Printed in Great Britain
by Amazon.co.uk, Ltd.,
Marston Gate.